THINK AND BE THIN

GRACE LIM

DEDICATION

This book is dedicated to everyone who wonders how to stay lean, strong and confident forever.

Table of Contents

ACKNOWLEDGMENTS

Thank you. Danke sehr. 谢谢 Xie xie.

Those two simple words in different languages represent much more than I can possibly express here. Those two words apply to many more people than I can possibly include here. Yet, I am deeply grateful for the events and the people that have been part of this journey.

Thank you to my hubby, Richard Lee. You were always there whenever I forgot to take my meal when I was busy writing this book. You took care of the house chores too.

This book could not have been written without the help and dedication of a team of fabulous people around me sharing their expertise and enthusiasm to create this book, especially NLAS Singapore.

A special thank-you to Dr. BJ Fogg, behavior scientist and innovator at Stanford University, author of Tiny Habits, for licensing approval to use the Fogg Behavior Model.

Thank you to my parents for believing in me and for supporting me no matter what. And last but not least, thank you to my siblings for their unconditional care for me.

Thank you, Lord, for your blessings and good health. Amen!

FOREWORD

Health is wealth. My beloved mum, aunt and mother-in-law all left me too early due to chronic disease – cancer. That is why I made the choice to live my life as healthy as I could.

We always want the best for our family. How are we going to give the best when we are not even taking good care of ourselves?

What is happiness when we are bedridden, unable to travel with our loved ones? What is happiness when we need to see our beloved suffer while taking care of us? Self-love is relatively important to keep us going and achieving what we want in life.

We all know that shedding some pounds will make us healthier, feel better, look better and maybe even live longer. Yet at every step of the way, things seem to go wrong.

Most of us just can't seem to make it to the gym, and you keep finding yourself with a cookie in our hand, even though you know better. We may even be aware of the fact that something is conflicting with what we "want," but we do not know what it is or where it came from, even if it's based upon false beliefs.

You can find the answers in this book! This is not a diet book. It focuses on your health, not your weight.

I got to know Grace as a Food Safety Management System consultant. She is also an NLP certified practitioner, as well as a nutrition coach, and her passion is to inspire everyone to have good health. She highlights about having our mind, soul and body treated as one when it comes to staying healthy.

Train your mind so you can communicate with your mind and tell it the healthy weight or dream body you want; you'll then get what you want. This applies to every aspect of your life.

Grace highly suggests that everyone can be healthy and have low risk in disease if we practice a healthy lifestyle – mentally and physically, being healthy from inside out. "Take care of your body. It's the only place you have to live." – Jim Rohn. I totally agree!

You are what you eat! In this book, Grace shares about making healthy food tasty. I can't wait to share this with more people! Eating nutritious food should be simple and easy. The most exciting part is, she told me there are 29 yummy healthy recipes in this book.

Samantha Mah, Co-Founder & Marketing Director of Love

FOREWORD

I recently met a woman who suffered from terrible knee pain whenever she walked. Pain induced by something as essential as walking is hard and tragic for anyone. The culprit was that her knees had become badly worn out from absorbing the excessive weight on her body.

When people think of a weight problem, they often think of their looks. In reality, weight problems affect almost every organ of their body as well. When you are overweight, your heart, bones, joints, and even your mental health is affected in various ways. This is why the World Health Organization has created programs that focus solely on helping you meet your ideal weight. Obesity has become so prevalent that it is now a national epidemic in countries like the United States.

The good news is that you are surrounded by many possible solutions. Just check out Amazon, and you will be flooded with authors of weight loss books. However, not all these authors are experts. The best experts are those who possess the academic and scientific background to their solution, went through the problem of weight loss, and actually corrected it. These experts experienced what you experienced and went through the ordeals you are going through. These experts know your challenges and have creatively found ways to help you solve them.

Grace Lim is an example of such an expert. She possesses impressive credentials, actively displays the mastery of the subject, and successfully overcame the challenges of weight loss. This is why she can understand what you are going through. The techniques she employs go beyond what is simply logical or scientific. They are practical and effective.

The system that Grace employs in this book is her own development, and it is medically sound. Reading her story inspired me further to work harder for my own health. I was so happy to read through this book not only because it is thorough in its execution, but it contains good advice on just about every aspect of weight loss you need.

Grace works hard to lose her own weight, and she works even harder to help others to do the same. It is her mission to help you to get a lean, strong and confident body using a powerful and sustainable system. May this book be the start of your amazing experience in weight loss. May this book and Grace's coaching help you achieve good results and good health.

Charles Edward Florendo, MD, DFM, FBPI, FIAMS
Family Physician and Buteyko Method Practitioner
Chief of Clinics, Mary Chiles Gen. Hospital, Manila

PREFACE

In year 2000, I embarked on a journey that would last more than two decades. I didn't know it then, but through a process of understanding the mind-body connection, I shed 10 kilogram or 22 pounds, and I have kept it off for twenty-one years, even up to the extent of having a 24-inch waistline.

Being actively involved in the learning and development industry for more than a dozen years, I hold a master's degree in health and safety from the University Malaya, Malaysia. I studied the psychology of eating from Harvard Extension School, United States. I'm a certified nutrition coach from Venice Nutrition, United States, a Human Resource Development Corporation certified professional trainer, a neuro linguistic programing certified practitioner, and a member of the Center of Mindful Eating USA. My ultimate mission is to help people to get a lean, strong and confident body using the honest and sustainable Think and Be T.H.I.N. Transformation Blueprint:

T- Think (Train Your Mind Thin)
H- Hybrid HIIT (Exercise Yourself Thin)
I- Survival Instinct (Learn Your Way Thin)
N- Nutrition (Eat Your Way Thin)

There are a million different diets out there promising everything from quick-and-easy weight loss to everlasting youth, and the sheer amount of advice can be overwhelming. Where do you start? How do you know which ones really work, so that you don't end up buying into a fad and wasting your time, or even risking your life trying out edible weight loss products, or wasting your hard-earned money on advanced technology such as liposuction?

This book describes the T.H.I.N. Transformation Blueprint I follow today, the most current evolution of a mental and physical quest that has made me 12 years younger than my chronological age. It is the approach that has transformed my life.

It works for me. And it will work for you.

Your journey to better health is not about a quick fix; it's about a lifestyle change that works for you. It's not about how quickly you can lose weight or how small you can become. It's about how to become stronger and healthier. With the Think and Be T.H.I.N. Transformation Blueprint, I will give you the tools you need to achieve your healthy weight or your dream physique.

Train Your Mind, Your Body Will Follow – Unknown

Think (Train Your Mind Thin) – Train your mind to change your life. I use a series of mindset tools to help you to learn more about yourself to set and achieve goals that will help you redefine your health and life. You do not need to use all the tools; my intention is to provide you multiple choices that fit into your lifestyle. And I'll share some famous and inspiring quotes to help you get stronger and more confident in your physical, intellectual, emotional, and spiritual health.

Hybrid HIIT (Exercise Yourself Thin) – My self-created program incorporates the latest science study on improving metabolism, burning fat, and maximizing your effort so every workout counts. You can even watch me demonstrating these moves for you in a series of easy-to-follow videos you'll find on http://www.thinkandbethin.com/

Survival Instinct (Learn Your Way Thin) – Become the expert of your body and its hunger signals. You are the best person — the only person — to make those choices. Essentially, it's the opposite of a traditional diet. It doesn't impose guidelines about what to avoid and what or when to eat.

Nutrition (Eat Your Way Thin) – I will show you the basics of the most important weight-loss hacks that nobody will tell you. You can be your own chef and eat real food. I will share with you my Y.U.M. (Yummy Unprocessed Meal) recipes (I'm not a fan of red meat, so you won't find any red meat recipes). No calorie counting, no weighing food, no diets, no rabbit food only. Eat all your favorite food. I really mean it—any food. Get the pictures of the Y.U.M. recipes on http://www.thinkandbethin.com/

We are on a journey, not a destination.
A journey to a leaner you.
A journey to a stronger you.
A journey to a more confident you.

Most importantly, a journey towards better physical, intellectual and emotional health.

I'm going to be with you the whole way no matter where you are! This I promise you!

Grace   Your   Body | Grace   Your   Life

DISCLAIMER

Neither the publisher nor the author is engaged in rendering professional advice or services to the individual reader. The ideas, procedures, and suggestions contained in this book are not intended as a substitute for consulting with your physician. All matters regarding your health require consulting with your physician. All matters regarding your health require medical supervision. Neither the publisher nor the author shall be liable or responsible for any loss or damage allegedly arising from any information or suggestion in this book.

The recipes container in this book have been created for the ingredients and techniques indicated. The publisher is not responsible for your specific health or allergy needs that may require supervision. Nor is the publisher responsible for any adverse reactions you may have to the recipes contained in the book, whether you follow them as written or modify them to suit your personal dietary needs or tastes.

INTRODUCTION

Who Is This Book For?

This book is for chronic dieters. This book is for people who are ready to learn why their diets haven't worked, and why what we've been taught about food and health hasn't worked. It's for people who have spent years going from diet to diet hoping that the next one would be the answer.

This book is not for people who feel perfectly fine with the way they eat, exercise, and relate to their body and weight; they probably don't need this book. But for those of you who are sick of being stuck in an abusive relationship with diets, who want a different lifestyle change, who want to cultivate good habits for being healthier and for longevity, this book is here to tell you there is a way out.

This book can benefit any person, of any gender, at any weight, who struggles with food and body image.

The reason the Think and Be T.H.I.N. Transformation Blueprint works with no restrictive diet or diet pills is because it tackles the most important part of the human: the mind. The mind keeps people falling off the wagon, and at the exact same time, exercise, nutritional knowledge, and survival instinct that we become obsessed with food and weight in the first place.

Why I Wrote This Book

This book is about giving you the information and experiences that cover complete wellness. But to be clear, between the ages of fifteen and twenty, I tried just every style of eating and exercise known to man.

Think and Be T.H.I.N. describes more than just my diet and fitness program; it describes the importance of a mindset that brought me some things that are more important: health, happiness and a deeper appreciation for the simple things in life. And that's what I want to share with you. Yes, the exercise program in this book will boost your metabolism, shrink and tone your body, and give you more energy than you've ever had. But it will give you something even more powerful: the confidence to set new goals – and to truly achieve them.

The U.S. weight loss market is now worth a record $72 billion with diet soft drinks, artificial sweeteners, health clubs, commercial diet center chains, multi-level marketing diet plans, OTC meal replacements and diet pills, medical programs (weight loss surgery, MDs, hospitals/clinic programs, Rx diet drugs, bariatricians, VLCD programs), low-cal frozen entrees, and the diet books and exercise DVDs market. However, 95% of diets fail. These highly desirable, fast, all-in approaches can shift the pounds on the scale quite drastically for the short term, but then the weight comes back even more. Think and Be T.H.I.N. Transformation Blueprint is a slower yet sustainable health-driven approach to change your lifestyle, and it doesn't have an endpoint, and it doesn't use the scale as the sole judge of success. No million-dollar paycheck required.

I began drafting the Think and Be T.H.I.N. plan in late 2018 while juggling my full-time nine-to-five job. At the end of 2020 during the height of the pandemic, I was working from home so that I got more time to write this book. One of the earliest lessons I learned was this: the most powerful thing about you is your mind. That's what makes this book different; conventional wisdom has always said that in order to lose weight, you need to eat less and move more. But skyrocketing obesity rates tell us that it's not that simple. Yes, in this book, I'm going to share with you about nutrition and exercise to reshape your physique, but most importantly, I'm going to share with you the techniques and tools to work on your mind to keep you great in all aspects of your life, including your physical and mental health, and perhaps it will work for your relationships as well.

The Think and Be T.H.I.N. Transformation Blueprint at a Glance

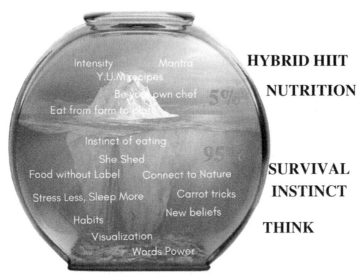

T.H.I.N TRANSFORMATION BLUEPRINT

Think (Train Your Mind Thin)

We all are creatures of habit, and the biggest habit of all is our way of thinking. Our life is the results of our actions, and our actions come from our thoughts, and our thoughts come from our beliefs. If we think we are not motivated enough, not smart enough, not good enough, then our actions will reflect those beliefs. This mindset will reflect in your actions and in the results of your day-in, day-out life.

Do you wake up every morning feeling energized, powerful, and excited about the day ahead? Or do you wake up feeling as tired as the night before? Will your current lifestyle make you a statistic? In the United States, someone has a heart attack every 40 seconds. To borrow a phrase from the seventeenth-century physician Thomas Moffett, we are "digging our graves with our teeth," as we cram our bodies with high-fat, nutritionally empty processed foods, and as we poison our body systems with cigarettes, alcohol, and drugs, and sit passively in front of our laptops. We all have dreams; we all feel we are destined for something bigger. You can only accomplish greatness with good health and a body that radiates vitality for you to go through the day. Think and Be T.H.I.N. Transformation Blueprint will guide you to the state of mind to do all those things. To get what we truly want, we have to go deeper.

I'll be sharing the techniques and tools to work on your subconscious mind for instant results.

Hybrid HIIT (Exercise Yourself Thin)

I train in the gym as well as at home. Most of the time, I run on roads or trails, and I have recently started to integrate HIIT into my exercise regimen. My personal coach helps me, especially with trail runs. I have been an athlete since my youth, so I love to invent new things to experience different results.

This 12-week program starts off moderately challenging, and the level of difficulty increases from there. Each workout is designed to take between 20 and 25 minutes (if you are elite, it will only take you 10 minutes), except for the "long course," which will take between 30 and 45 minutes.

Each week will include:
3 Cardio sessions
1 Upper body workout
1 Lower body workout
1 Abs workout
1 Long circuit

Your schedule could be something like this. Play around with the schedule to suit your preference.

MON	TUE	WED	THUR	FRI	SAT	SUN
Upper body (P.M.)	Cardio 1 (A.M.) Lower body (P.M.)	Cardio 2 (A.M.) Abs (P.M.)	Cardio 3 (A.M. or P.M.)	Off	Long circuit (A.M. or P.M.)	Off

There are two workouts on some of the days; the main purpose is to boost your metabolism. Some of the days we strike to the max, some of the days are easy; this is to work on your mindset as well. We tend to not do things if they are always hard.

Some of the days are without resting times, so you are going to push through those limitations and get stronger over time. Push through this mindfully.

Always listen to your body. If you feel pain at your knees, hips, elbows or shoulders, you might need to modify the workout. If running outdoors is not feasible because of rain, you can switch to a treadmill or indoor bike riding. Be flexible.

Survival Instinct (Learn Your Way Thin)

The word "instinct" is an innate, hardwired tendency. For example, humans have biological, hardwired instincts for survival—behaviour that is mediated by reactions below the conscious level. The instinct of eating is about listening to your body's own cues to decide what, when, and how much to eat. The instinct of eating is not a science; it is an art and a practical practice to turn into one's inner knowing. Eat whatever you want. Your choices are affected by your preferences and by your awareness and degree of concern about nutrition information, as well as what foods are available. You naturally seek balance, assortment and moderation in your eating. You don't use rigid rules to decide what to eat; therefore, you don't judge yourself for what you eat. Eating is usually pleasurable, but food doesn't hold any particular power over you.

As I promise, this is not a normal diet book! (This is indeed an anti-diet book.)

Nutrition (Eat Your Way Thin)

You may find this eating plan quite unique because it only focuses on eating REAL food! REAL food is food that has less than 3 ingredients. Furnish yourself with the basic knowledge of nutrition and influence your decision making when it comes to choosing the right quality food to put into your mouth. You will then understand restrictive diet causing nutrition deficiency follows by lifestyle illnesses.

Number of Meals
Three per day: Breakfast, lunch and dinner

Number of Snacks
Two or three per day (sometimes I snack during the night time)

Avoid? Cut Down On?
Just eat mindfully; your mind will tell you what to avoid.

Calories?
Eat mindfully and you will eventually choose the right food with the right calories, and the calories will take care of themselves.

Avoid Hunger
Don't starve yourself in order to lose weight. You might notice this meal plan has no food restrictions. You might be asking, how can this result in weight loss? Eating the right food at the right time is the most effective weight-loss tool.

Sneak peek of the Y.U.M. recipes:

Breakfast/ Lunch/ Dinner	
Half-boiled eggs	Muesli or granola with Greek yogurt
Quinoa + millet porridge with dried scallops and dried oyster	Overnight oats
Millet pumpkin porridge	

Lunch/ Dinner	
Prawn aglio olio spaghetti	Tofu and kimchi stewed
Oven-baked salmon and asparagus	

Desserts	
Green beans with ginkgo	Tapioca cake
Sea coconut with dried longan	

MY TRANSFORMATION

As an ex-state badminton player, I was trained by a coach at the age of six. I was also a great volleyball player. I love other sports like sprinting and table-tennis as well. Growing up as a super active kid, sports was part of my everyday routine. For a farm girl or village girl like me, sports were the best leisure activity after school hours and free time. The word "DIETING" was never in my dictionary. I knew I could easily burn off the calories during my badminton training or other sports leisure time.

Due to my outstanding achievement in badminton, I was chosen by a famous reputable high school, aka badminton school, that sponsored badminton players for the state. I was super excited. The school was 40 kilometers away from my parents' house; therefore, I rented a room together with a senior who was also a badminton player and eventually met other new classmates. Renting a room meant there was no way to enjoy home cook meals. First, I enjoyed eating out, 3 meals a day in the food court and the school canteen. Once a week, I ate instant cup noodles.

I decided to focus on academics after seeing my poor results in my Lower Secondary Assessment (Malaysian Public Examination). At the age of 15, I stopped being active but continued eating the same way as I did when I was a competitive athlete, causing me to gain 10 kilograms. Ten kilograms is a big pack of rice, right? The worst thing was, I wasn't aware about the gain in my weight until one of my best friends thought I had a toothache because my face looked so swollen and puffy. I looked in the mirror at my face and body. Gosh!

Me in year 1995

From that moment, I set a goal. "I want to lose some weight." I wrote this on a paper and pasted it on the wall in my rented room. I went on diets and cleanses, I avoided entire food groups and skipped meals. I also started jogging regularly. Months passed, but nothing seemed to work for me. I was a little upset and didn't feel positive about it. Deep down, I didn't really believe I'd be able to slim down. I thought I was going to be in that body shape for the rest of my life.

My grandma had a huge body, so I figured it must be genetic.

I felt so uncomfortable with myself that it radiated to other aspects of my life. I didn't go out my friends because I knew they were going to eat out, and I was actively trying to avoid food.

I wouldn't want to go clothes shopping with my friends because I figured the nice and sexy dresses wouldn't fit me.

As a result of chronic dieting, these were the things I got:-
- Pimples
- Constipation
- Fatigue and dizziness
- Poor memories
- Depressed
- Low self-esteemed

I was in that situation for five years! Perhaps some of you can relate with this experience.

Until...........

One day, I remember it was a Saturday morning, I got off from the bus back to my parents' home. I bumped into my badminton coach, Gary. He was a bit shocked by my body's size. I told him, "I just can't see myself being slim." So, he asked me, "What would happen if you could see yourself being lean and fit?"

That was a light-bulb moment. I instantly created the picture of me being lean and fit in my mind. My face instantly brightened with big eyes and a wide smiling mouth, and I said of course I would love it.

He continued to say something along the lines of, "Just see yourself being in the size and shape that you want to be, and feel how good it would feel to see yourself looking good in the mirror and to hear appreciative comments from your friends about how good you look, as you feel lean and strong and confident."

He woke me up with this phrase, "Your mind and body are

connected." Everything that happens in the mind creates an effect in the body. Sometimes, these changes are too small to notice, but with a deep mental action follows a strong physical reaction. This may manifest within the nervous system. Or it means the way you think will determine the results you get.

"What I hear, I forget.
What I see, I remember.
What I do, I understand." – Chinese proverb

He told me to spend some about 5 to 10 minutes in the next few days visualizing myself being the size and shape I wanted to be, and then to feel it, see it and hear it.

A few months later, I was back in my "athlete" body shape, and I have kept it for 20 years to this day. In the morning after waking up and at night time before going to bed, I did a visualization exercise for 10 minutes. I continued to exercise regularly and to eat healthily. If you have heard of neuro linguistic programming (NLP), you know that visualization is one of its powerful tools. NLP is also used by psychologists as a successful therapy for treating eating disorders. In 2018, I got myself certified as an NLP practitioner. I picked up more NLP tools to further strengthen my overall health, physically and mentally. I will share with you all I have learned in this book.

I am now in my late 30s. I have 11 lines in my abdominal muscles without working on it. I do mostly road running and trail running and of course hybrid HIIT, but I rarely focus on my abs. One fine evening, when I stood in front of the mirror, I saw the 11 lines and I was so excited. I always wanted tone-up abs! I couldn't agree more that it is the power of mind and body connection. At this stage, I think there is one more thing that is more important to me: I'm 12 years younger than my chronological age.

Me in Year 2020

Placebo Effect:

You've probably heard of the placebo effect. Under the right circumstances, the brain can convince the body that a fake treatment is the real thing. Check out the reference; it's in the 1981 World Journal of Surgery. Scientists were testing a new chemotherapy. It was an injectable substance that was given to two groups of patients. One group of patients received the actual chemotherapy, and the other group of patients received a placebo, meaning a fake, harmless, inert chemical substance, which in this case was water.

Why do we even give a placebo? Because if you truly want to understand the efficacy of a new prescription drug, pharmaceutical companies must test these against placebos because in approximately 50% of all cases, on average, you can get as much benefit or more from a placebo than the actual drug itself. That's a mind-bending statistic, by the way. After a number of weeks, for the patients who received the real chemotherapy, 100% of them had a very common side effect – they all lost their hair. And 31% of the patients on the placebo chemotherapy also had a very interesting side effect – they, too, lost their hair. Now all they were doing was getting an injection of water and somehow, their hair fell out.

Why would they lose their hair? Well, according to what we know about placebo science, those people likely had the association "have cancer, go on chemotherapy, lose hair." If the power of the mind is that strong that you could take a water injection, think it's going to make you lose your hair, and you do lose it, what happens when you say, "I just can't see myself being slim," or, "It must be genetic"?

The human nervous system is goal-seeking, and it will move towards whatever goals you put into it. The goal I had been using was "I want to lose some weight." This presents two problems:

a) I was saying what I didn't want (weight) instead of what I did want.

Your subconscious mind does not process negatives directly. In order to process negation, the subconscious has to think of it first. Do not slip! You would have to process slipping first, in order to even think of not slipping. (If I say, "Don't imagine a pink elephant," you have to imagine it to understand what I've said.) By setting goals as losing weight, I was having to represent the weight to myself in some way.

"What you resist persists. And only what you look at, and own, can disappear. You make it disappear by simply changing your mind about it." – Neale Donald Wasch

b) People don't like to lose things! We have been conditioned since we were children not to lose things, and if we do, to find them again.

Stating my goal in that way, coupled with fact that I didn't have a mental image of myself being lean, meant that I kept getting what I didn't want (my mental image was of me being the shape I already was).

Remember, my badminton coach asked me, "What would happen if you could see yourself being lean and fit?"

Instantly I created the picture of me being lean and sexy in my mind. My face instantly brightened with big eyes and a wide smiling mouth, and I said I would love it. Did you notice that the question instantly changed the feelings because during that moment, I changed my focus to the positive words that my badminton coach used and started to picture it? The words you habitually choose affect how you communicate with yourself and therefore the results you experience.

Remember, "A small tweak makes a huge difference."

Each word represents a small step towards cultivating the body you want. Medical doctors explain that words have extreme power, and how you use them shapes how you feel personally. Start paying attention to the words you use frequently and begin to see where patterns emerge in your thought processes, and change them if you need to.

Hence, the right phrase to communicate with your mind is, "I want to have a lean, strong and confident body." At the same time, you must be able to create the picture of you being lean and strong.

PART 1: THINK (TRAIN YOUR MIND THIN)

CHAPTER 1

RIVER OF THOUGHTS

It is very nice to think;
Every lady wishes to be thin.
It is common to overthink;
Along the journey to be thin.

WATCHING YOUR RIVER OF THOUGHTS

There are lots of incredible things about us humans, and one of the most fascinating things is our ability to observe what is going on in our mind. There is no other species that can do that. Not only can we know what is going on in our mind, but we can step back from it and observe ourselves as we are in the process of knowing! The only person who has the ability to read your mind and change your mind is you. You may come across people asking, "Can people read each other's mind?" Research suggests that our discernment of others' emotions and trustworthiness may manifest in our body's reactions to them, at least as strongly as in our mental assessments of their speech. Trusting one's gut, then, by being mindful of our body's reactions to someone else, can help us make more accurate judgments about others.

Sound complicated? Well, it's actually really simple, and the best way to describe it is by bringing to mind an image of yourself sitting at the side of a river. As you look at this image in your mind's eye, you become an observer of yourself. You can see what is going on in the river, and you can see what you are doing as you sit there watching it.

The river contains (metaphorically) all the thoughts, ideas, stories and memories that are flowing through your mind. Occasionally, one of these thoughts will pop up to the surface of the river, a bit like one of those flying fish that leaps out of the water. Sitting on the bank of the river, you notice these thoughts popping up, and what you can also notice is that they float on the surface for a while then they disappear of their own accord.

The mind is like a river. The thoughts are like various droplets of water. We are submerged in that water. Stay on the bank and watch your mind. – A.G. Mohan

The river is constantly flowing and therefore constantly changing. This is just like the activity in our mind. Thoughts come and go. They appear without us asking them to (and sometimes they can be really random), and they also disappear without us needing to do anything.

In life, if your thoughts are always pointing toward the negative and repeatedly pondering your own shortcomings, dwelling on your failure, or seeing the obstacles up ahead of you, you will inevitably crash right into them.

I love to think of it this way: Our negative thoughts are like sediment; this refers to the conglomerate of materials, organic and inorganic, that can be carried away by the river, for example, clay, silt and sand. When we think negative thoughts about ourselves or others, we are building up the layers of sediment, and scientifically, it becomes sedimentary rocks, affecting water flowing in the river. We get stuck in that negative space and keep manifesting the negative thoughts.

"Your beliefs become your thoughts,
Your thoughts become your words,
Your words become your actions,
Your actions become your habits,
Your habits become your values,
Your values become your destiny." – Mahatma Gandhi

What if, instead of getting caught up in a pattern of negative thoughts, you refocused your energy and developed empowering habits that utilize positive thinking? By training your mind to block negative thoughts with positive thinking, you're steadily training yourself to stop thinking in a negative way. Fear won't rule you anymore. That's the power of positive thinking.

It starts with your river of thoughts.

"Thoughts rule the world." – Ralph Waldo Emerson

THE 95/5 RULE OF T.H.I.N.

I remember I read an article from Forbes, and they were using a fantastic metaphor to describe our conscious and subconscious mind. It went like this:

Have you ever wanted to drive a Lamborghini? Imagine the speed, the ease of handling, the wind through your hair.

Compare that to being on a skateboard, moving under your own steam. It takes effort, only goes fast in short bursts, is unpredictable and not great on handling. You're exposed, dependent on the terrain and weather conditions.

Which would you rather drive?

Let's call the Lamborghini your subconscious mind and the skateboard is part of your conscious mind. One is powerful, present and has you arriving in style; the other is slow and clunky and maybe gets you there in the end. Which one is driving you? I believe you have got the answer. Yes, your subconscious mind, where you store your old beliefs, is powerful.

Self-development author Brian Tracy summarizes the importance of the subconscious mind: "Let's first take a moment to consider the fact that your subconscious mind is like a huge memory bank. Its capacity is virtually unlimited, and it permanently stores everything that ever happens to you. By the time you reach the age of 21, you've already permanently stored more than one hundred times the contents of the entire Encyclopaedia Britannica. The function of your subconscious mind is to store and retrieve data. Its job is to ensure that you respond exactly the way you are programmed. Your subconscious mind makes everything you say and do fit a pattern consistent with your self-concept, your 'master program.' This is why repeating positive affirmations is so effective—you can actually reprogram your own thought patterns by slipping in positive and success-oriented sound bites."

When you fall asleep, it is your conscious mind that is sleeping. However, your subconscious mind will never fall asleep. It works 24 hours a day, even when you sleep. Your subconscious mind is controlling your body, your breathing, your organ functionality, your cell growth and everything. This is why when you sleep, your subconscious mind is still wide awake.

This is the point where your subconscious mind connects with your mental images that produce, what we call, dreams. And because our subconscious mind thinks in the form of symbols, metaphors, and visual forms, our dreams tend to be projected in that way too. This is why most dreams are indirect and difficult to understand, but they are often connected to our experiences and the events in our daily life.

Your subconscious mind does everything to move you towards pleasure and away from pain. It is highly influenced by the words and pictures you put in your mind, loves what is familiar and prefers to avoid anything unfamiliar. As long as you believe that chocolate and candy or burgers and fries or pizza makes you happy and helps you to cope and is a reward, then you are linking pleasure to these things and will probably crave them during times of stress. Since you can choose what to link pain and pleasure to, link pleasure to refusing chocolate, pizza and fries. Link pleasure to looking great on the beach and remind yourself that eating healthy food in the right amounts is what really helps you to cope with stress and is a better reward for your body. Making the right choices and changing your beliefs will make you more successful at getting your lean, strong and confident body.

When you are specific and communicate with your subconscious mind using detailed words that give your mind the right message and the right images, any misinterpretation is less likely to happen, and that is exactly what will happen to you as you follow this exciting program. If you want to be fit and healthy, you must say to your mind, "I have chosen to eat fruit instead of dessert, and I have chosen to feel great about that because I have chosen to be a size S."

This is a clear instruction to your mind, whereas saying, "I want pizza, but I can't have it because I am on diet," only increases and intensifies the desire for pizza. Your subconscious mind is much more powerful than your conscious mind so you must use that power for your benefit. Understanding how your subconscious mind works will help you to positively influence your mind, rather than being influenced by thoughts, beliefs, and behaviors that you do not want and grew out of years ago.

"An enormous portion of cognitive activity is non-conscious; figuratively speaking, it could be 95 percent. We probably will never know precisely how much is outside awareness." – Emanual Donchin, American neuroscientist

In other words, 95% of our brain's activity happens on the subconscious level.

So why is knowing the 95/5 ratio essential to get thin?

According to Theory of Mind by Dr. Kappas, the subconscious controls everything in our lives, like our beliefs, habits, behaviors, emotions and feelings, relationship patterns, addictions, creativity, intuition, involuntary body functions, spiritual connection, developmental stages and long-term memory.

Now imagine your doctor said it was time for you to lose some weight. In your conscious mind, you know that is a good idea. You will be healthier, feel better, look better and maybe even live longer. Yet at every step of the way, things seem to go wrong. You just can't seem to make it to the gym, and you keep finding yourself with a cookie in your hand, even though you know better. You may even be aware of the fact that something is conflicting with what you "want," but you do not know what it is or where it came from, or even if it's based upon false beliefs.

It's not enough for your conscious mind to want to change. The subconscious will win every time. Remember, the subconscious likes "knowns," even if they are negative. To it, the gym is scary. It's an unknown (you may not be active for decades). It would rather stick with the status quo than take a risk with that unknown. As for eating, those cookies have definite positive associations in the subconscious. It's going to want more. The belief that cookies are good in the subconscious mind far outweighs the conscious desire to look and feel better by doing something like eating a green salad.

By default, the subconscious is slow to change. If you can keep a sustained effort going, it is possible, but that is sheer willpower at work. Unfortunately, most people will fail. Beliefs embedded in the modern memory will keep sabotaging the desire of the conscious mind.

What if you know how to communicate with your subconscious mind effectively and insert a few positive associations in place of the negatives and unknowns you have about losing weight and going to the gym? In the same way that the conscious mind will always lose in a "tug-of-war" with the subconscious mind, it can't lose when both parts are united.

This is what I call "The 95/5 Rule of T.H.I.N."

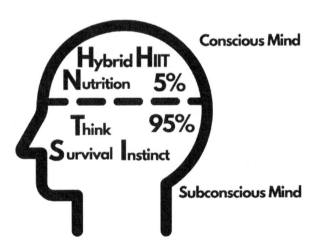

The 95/5 Rule of T.H.I.N

Worksheet: River of Thoughts

Describe yourself in one word:

_____

The most important thing in my life is:

_____

If I could do any job, it would be:

_____

CHAPTER 2

COMMUNICATE WITH YOUR SUBCONSCIOUS MIND

Do you see what I see?
Do you believe what I believe?
You'll see it when you believe it.
You'll get it when you see it.

VISUALIZE YOURSELF THIN

Download the guided visualization audio at
http://www.thinkandbethin.com/

Train your mind so you can reach and maintain your healthy weight forever more easily than you thought possible. You probably heard about this when many people talk about manifest or law of attraction to get wealthy. Not many people will tell you visualization helps you to get thin. When you can visualize yourself as thin and as someone who effortlessly and naturally makes the right food choices, then you are one step closer to achieving your healthy weight. The reason you need to train your mind to visualize yourself as thin is because your body will act in a way that matches your thinking. This is not about you thinking yourself thin, but you never move your ass and you keep feeding yourself empty foods.

One thing we know for sure is that our subconscious mind obeys our thoughts and brings forth what we want through the projection of thoughts. We often hear the words, "We are what we think," or "We become who we think about most of the time" because thoughts are energy and our subconscious mind transforms them into reality.

"Anything you can imagine, you can create." – Oprah Winfrey

Do not confuse daydreaming with visualizing.

Everyone has the capacity to daydream. But here's the catch - it's random by its very nature. It happens unexpectedly, and there's usually no specific purpose behind it. Images come and go as they please, often without any logical connection.

Visualization, however, is not random. It's not unexpected. It's usually undertaken with a definite purpose or goal in mind before you begin. Images will still come and go, but now you're focusing on those images, on their relationship to each other, and on their significance to your underlying goal or purpose.

The strongest and most powerful force in your subconscious mind is its need to act in a way that matches your thinking. This means your body responds to the pictures you are making in your mind and the words you are speaking or thinking, and it works continuously to make those pictures and words your reality. Your subconscious mind does not reason things out; it just believes whatever you tell it, so telling yourself you can never lose weight or you can't stick to any diet or that ice cream is your downfall simply makes it more likely that this will always be your reality. As you learn that you act in a way that is 100% consistent with the way you define yourself, you can then understand that changing your thinking comes before changing your eating. Ninety-five percent of this program is going to do all this for you so it's easier and becomes who you are rather than what you do.

Athletes will imagine that they are making the perfect shot or performing at their best to win the championship. They practice this visualization in their head every day. And eventually, their mind will perform exactly like how they have visualized and bring them the result they want.

Visualization is the simplest way to communicate with your subconscious mind. If you are a parent with kids, think about how you use visual aids like flash cards to teach your kids when they first learn.

"It all depends on what you visualize." – Ansel Adams

Your mind always influences your body, and you in turn can influence your mind by using the things that influence your subconscious. These are your powers of visualization and your ability to see yourself differently to let your mind know what it is that you really want and desire. Once accepted, these ideas create the same reactions in the body again and again; that's the mind body connection. Therefore, weight loss really can be effortless.

Three Steps to Visualize Yourself Thin

1. Practice visualization is first thing to do once u wake up in the morning, spend 5 to 10 minutes, sit comfortably on the floor or chair in a place without distraction, and start to visualize yourself thin, you may play some relaxing music which can gear you toward focusing on your visualization.

Note 1: Make visualization your daily practice. This will eventually become your habits if you practice it consistently.

Note 2: If you find that visualization is difficult, one of the ways you can train your mind to see yourself thin is to find a picture of you when you were slimmer as this will remind your mind that 'If you were like that once, you can be like that again.' Alternatively, you could find a picture of someone with the body type that you would like to look like.

2. While staring at the picture, tell yourself this "I have the power to create the body I desire."

3. Close your eyes and imagine that you look exactly like the picture. Imaging you are doing something healthy like exercising or eating salad in that body type that you want. Every time you visualize:
• Make the picture exciting and compelling.
• Increase the duration and intensity.
• Hold the picture for longer.
• Make it bigger, brighter and clearer.

You can practice this visualization any time. When you get yourself familiarize with it, and when you literally fall in love with it, it will be "saved" in your subconscious mind.

Fake it until you make it! If you can't imagine it, just imagine you can imagine it. Acting "as if" doesn't mean being phony or inauthentic. It's about changing yourself on the inside.

"Who you are inside is what helps you make and do everything in life." – Fred Rogers in The World According to Mister Rogers: Important Things to Remember.

There is plenty of science that proves you can actually fool yourself and others into becoming more successful, finding love, and increasing your happiness. Researchers have found that "acting" a certain way allows your brain to "rehearse" a new way of thinking and can set off a desired chain of events in the future.

Make visualization your habit. I will talk more about habit in next chapter.

Advanced Visualization

Humans have five basic senses: touch, sight, hearing, smell and taste. The sensing organs associated with each sense send information to the brain to help us understand and perceive the world around us.

Visual (sight)
Auditory (sound)
Kinesthetic (touch)

Olfactory (smell)
Gustatory (taste)

As visualization is only one of the senses, failing to utilize the other four senses in our visualization means that we are using only 20% of the mind's tools to work on our goal of being thin. What happens when you start using five senses in your visualization practice? Powerful stuff, right? You have to use the imagination; there's no other way.

I would like to invite all of you to experience the difference by utilizing your five senses.

If you are safe, close your eyes and take a moment to focus on your breathing, concentrating on slowing how you breathe. Now imagine you are in your kitchen. Familiarize yourself with the feel of it, the look of it, and even its smell. Take a minute or so over this. Visualize yourself going to wherever you would keep a lemon in the kitchen; take a knife and cut the lemon in half. Once you have done this, vividly imagine raising the lemon to your face and smelling it. Then bite down on it and squeeze all its juice into your mouth. Now pause; are you making faces? Are you salivating? Your mind doesn't know the difference between imagination and reality. This exercise also demonstrates how your mind will respond to what you visualize with the other four senses as though it were real.

"Imagination is more important than knowledge." – Albert Einstein

For example, I used to visualize myself running on the beach. See yourself in your dream body shape and imagine your body in the scene. You see the white sand, the zephyr-haunted cliffs and a wide slash of the bay. You hear the snoozy sea lap gently. The sun is toasting your skin like nuts in the oven. The sea air smells of chlorine. The neon-blue sky is threaded with silver. See yourself in the scene. What do you look like? What do you feel, hear, and smell?

However, if you feel overwhelmed with this advanced visualization, don't worry. Just imagine yourself being thin in your own preferable way. It still works!

Download the visualization audio at http://www.thinkandbethin.com/

WORDS HAVE POWER

Words matter: The mere fact of speaking can have a strong influence on how you think. As we all know, "we are what we eat," but most of us don't know that "we are what we speak." Our words become our reality and our mind uses the words we speak to identify what we are feeling. Words you simply imagine in your mind can affect your brain functions. Your brain takes every word you say as literal and accurate. Negatives are processed differently by neurology than they are in words. Every day, numerous words pass through our stream of consciousness. By intervening in and altering the flow of that stream of self-talk, we can change our behaviors, our emotions, and even our physical health.

"A powerful agent is the right word. Whenever we come upon one of those intensely right words…..the resulting effect is physical as well as spiritual, and electrically prompt." – **Mark Twain**

Medical doctors explain that words have extreme power, and how you use them shapes how you feel personally. Start paying attention to the words you use frequently and begin to see where patterns emerge in your thought processes, and change them if you need to. To interrupt the patterns, you may use any ridiculous words you can. Here is a list of negative words/ phrases that I use, and many of my clients use. You can change them to any funny words/ phrases you can:

Negative	transform	Positive
Confuse	to	Curious
Failure	to	Learning
Lazy	to	Power charging
Lonely	to	Available
Afraid	to	Uncomfortable
Anxious	to	A little concerned
Depressed	to	Not on the top of it
Disappointed	to	Underwhelmed
Overwhelmed	to	In demand
Fearful	to	Curious
Nervous	to	Energized
Painful	to	Uncomfortable
Rejected	to	Misunderstood
Stupid	to	Unresourceful
Terrible	to	Different
Sick	to	Cleansing
I hate	to	I prefer
I am absolutely starving.	to	I need to eat something.
I could eat a horse.	to	I could eat now.
I will always be fat.	to	I am changing my shape and size.
I can't leave food.	to	I feel powerful when I
I am just an out-of-control pig.	to	I know what to do and how to do it now
I am the size of a house.	to	I am becoming leaner every day.
I eat as much as ten men.	to	I have a normal selective appetite.
I have to lose weight.	to	I have to let go of 10 pounds.
I am losing weight.	to	I am dropping weight.
I am trying to stay on the diet.	to	I will stay on this diet.
I wish I could be a size S.	to	I absolutely definitely will be a size S.
I dream of being thinner.	to	I can be thinner.
I hope I succeed this time.	to	I know I will succeed.

Many people find it helpful to write down negative words they find themselves using throughout the day. For every negative word, write a positive alternative next to it. Keep the alternatives in the back of your mind to use next time. If you find this aspect of powerful words overwhelming, start with just one area of your life that causes negative thoughts, like exercising. Catch yourself in those moments, and build from there.

Be Specific

To get your mind to do what you want it to, you must tell your mind what you want, and you must tell it using specific, descriptive words and images. "I want to be a size S, I want to look great in jeans or beachwear and I want to do whatever it takes to get there. I want to make healthier choices and to feel really good about those choices, and I want to exercise regularly and enjoy doing it." Give your mind this very clear message repeatedly by saying it and thinking it daily and by looking at your collage several times a day. This ensures that your mind clearly and specifically knows, without any misinterpretation, exactly what it is you want and therefore you are much more likely to get it.

Positivity Is Key

The way you feel about any situation is linked to only two things: the pictures you make in your head and the words you say to yourself. If your pictures and words are, "Cookies are yummy and super delicious. I love them and can't live without them," then you will find it so much harder to resist cookies. By changing the words to, "Cookies have refined fat and sugar that my body does not even want," then that's what you respond to instead. When you are in the cinema, they flash up images of food they want you to buy because they know you respond directly to those words and images. Do you know that you see and hear 1000 adverts every day asking you to eat junk and fast food? The food adverts on TV, on social media platforms, in magazines, on billboards and on the radio make you want the very food they are describing. Those adverts were designed to make you drool over the food and buy it, and they work because they influence the unconscious mind.

It's all up to you. Sometimes you can't control life's events, but you can control how you react to them. Once you empower yourself to change what's in your control, you can make this ability to influence your mind positively by filling up your mind with images of better, healthier food and telling yourself this is what you really want and crave. When you say things like, "I can't lose weight. I will never be a size S forever," you are forming an image that you eventually turn into. Your mind has no ability to disagree with whatever you tell it, so you will become much more successful at losing weight when you tell yourself better things, and not just occasionally but all the time.

Think of someone who's had a profound impact on your life. It can be a close friend, family member or someone you've never met, like a celebrity, professional athlete or renowned entrepreneur. What mottos does that person live by? Have they been able to unlock extraordinary things in their lives due to their positive thinking habits?

Chances are, they use the power of positive thinking to find the success they seek, and you can, too. When you feel yourself falling into negative habits, pull up a quotation or positive affirmation from someone you respect. Read it and determine how you can best embody it. You can even write it down and post it somewhere you'll see it often, such as on the refrigerator or on the side of your computer screen or make it your computer's wallpaper.

"If you have good thoughts they will shine out of your face like sunbeams, and you will always look lovely," – Roald Dahl

Three Steps to Collect Your Powerful Words

1. Keep a mini note with you, write down your negative words throughout the day. There's something about taking a negative word out of your head and putting it onto paper (or screen) that takes a little weight off your shoulders.

2. For every negative word, write a positive alternative next to it.

3. Keep the alternatives in the back of your mind to use next time.

FORM NEW BELIEFS

You can't form new beliefs and harness the power of positive thinking if you're unaware of your current ones (limiting beliefs). In actual fact, most of these beliefs are not true, but if you continue to talk about yourself like this, then you are continuing to be a part of the problem instead of being part of the solution. Even if they were true, you can change a belief which in turn can change your mind to change your body, because our beliefs affect the physiological processes in our bodies.

According to Anthony Robbins in his book, Awaken the Giant Within, "Most of our beliefs are generalizations about our past, based on out interpretations of painful and pleasurable experiences. The challenge is threefold: 1. Most of us do not consciously decide what we're going to believe; 2. Often our beliefs are based on misinterpretation of past experiences; and 3. Once we adopt a belief, we forget it's merely an interpretation." Every thought we think creates a physical change in our bodies.

"Whether you think you can or think you can't, you're right." – Henry Ford

We all have a voice inside our head that speaks to us. This voice gets louder and stronger, especially when we are faced with taking on a new challenge or stepping out of our comfort zone. This is because when we seek to change, we face uncertainty, and with uncertainty comes fear. Getting up and doing something is hard; you don't know if you are going to reach your goal. When your inner critic Finds Excuses And Reasons (F.E.A.R.), it becomes tougher.

Excuses
The inner critic will tend to say things to you like this:

I don't have time
I'm too tired
The gym is too far

It's okay to skip just one day

Or on a deeper level:

I am not capable of achieving this
I gain weight easily
I can't trust my body
People will laugh at me

The thing is that often, the deeper level beliefs will not always be obvious, and the mind will use the list of excuses as an easier way of getting out of something rather than facing up to the real underlying root cause of the problem. This is the inner critic that will stop you before you even begin. You have to learn how to become aware of this voice and shut down the thoughts as they happen. Learn how to call out the lies so they don't control your actions.

Remember, if you're overeating on a regular basis, the real cause is usually a belief problem rather than a problem with food itself. Therefore, it is very important to study your limiting beliefs you might have if you want to success in all aspects of your life, physical health, mental health and relationships. If you never address them all the techniques in the world won't matter.

Positive thinking bypasses that rage and inconvenience, allowing you to just enjoy the moment and be fully present. By consciously choosing to focus on positive moments in your life, you'll begin to reframe your thoughts, cultivating a mindset that is grateful and open rather than negative and closed off. And those beliefs affect your life and your happiness.

Reframing to Shift Old Beliefs Instantly

Reframing is a cognitive technique that can be used to blast those limiting beliefs into oblivion. It can be used to destroy both limiting beliefs and ones that are just starting to form inside your mind. In fact, it can become a very powerful tool to learn to recognize a limiting belief in the making. When your inner critic is in the progress to Find Excuses And Reasons (F.E.A.R.), use reframing to prevent it from gaining foothold.

Eventually, reframing means consciously questioning the belief you have created. If you doubt about a belief that you have and apply reframing to it, you'll notice that the belief is most likely irrational and cannot be true, so why not just abandon it? After all, you are a rational person, aren't you?

Being able to reframe your limiting beliefs can improve the experience of getting lean from being one you hate to one you actually enjoy.

Let's look at this:

Excuse: I don't have time to exercise.

That's the most common answer given when asked why people don't exercise regularly. Nobody has enough time. People don't skip out on exercise because they don't think it's good for them. People don't exercise because they'd rather be doing something else.

Question: So, do you really ever have "no time" for exercise?

Of course not. You can always find time for exercise, but only if it's a priority. Let's just be honest here: checking your Facebook newsfeed IS often more important/valuable/enjoyable than exercising. The stats are very clear that this is true.

Reframe to New Belief: I make time to move my body.

Movement is what your body needs. The term "exercise" might conjure up images of high-intensity workout, running on a treadmill, or lifting weights in the gym. These are all great BUT they are not the solution to the exercise problem for most people. Start with body movement like stretching, and when time goes by, increase the intensity.

Once you have reframed your limiting beliefs, take committed action. Committed action is exhibited when an individual consistently demonstrates the specific behaviors needed to result in optimal performance

"There is a difference between interested and committed. When you're interested, you do it when it's convenient. When you're committed to something, you accept no excuses, only results." – Ken Blanchard

Compared to the limiting beliefs, how much more powerful would the new beliefs support you? Just like in order to succeed, we need to be open to receiving success, to form new beliefs, you need to be open for new input and make room for new beliefs.

You need to believe you can get over it, get through it, get to the body that you really want.

Making the Unfamiliar (New Beliefs) Familiar

Your mind loves and wants to return to what is familiar. Therefore, to achieve real and lasting success at becoming and staying slimmer, you must work at making the familiar unfamiliar and the unfamiliar familiar. The mind loves what is familiar and wants to keep going there, but to succeed at weight loss, you have to make the familiar unfamiliar and the unfamiliar familiar. If you never exercise, and if what is familiar is lounging around eating packets of chips or cookies, it will feel unfamiliar to go to the gym, but when you go enough, then exercise becomes familiar and lounging around becomes unfamiliar. If you have coffee with full fat milk and sugar, then that is familiar; coffee with skimmed milk and no sugar is unfamiliar, but stick with it and it will become so familiar that if you try it the old way, it tastes horrible. Only having desserts occasionally instead of every time you eat out becomes familiar, as you realize that you have the power to make good habits a part of your life and bad habits history

Three Steps to Form New Beliefs

1. Recognise your limiting beliefs, think about all the excuses and reasons you have about why you will not be able to lose weight is about losing weight and how you learnt them.
2. Reframe and replace your limiting belief with new belief that gives

you power.
3. Take committed action.

Worksheet: Communicate with Your Subconscious Mind

When was the last time you did a body checkup?

_____

What do you want to weigh? What size do you want to be?

_____

Do you have a picture of yourself being the weight/ size you want to be? Use the "Three Steps to Visualize Yourself Thin."

_____

What are the limiting beliefs that stopping you from achieving your dream body? Use the "Three Steps to Form New Beliefs."

_____

CHAPTER 3

CREATURES OF HABITS

You want a better future for a better life?
You gotta work on your habits now.
You decide your habits.
Your habits decide your future.

When was the last time you made a resolution? I am going to eat healthier. I am going to work out every day. I am going to sleep early. For a time, we work out, swap vegetables for fries, and make sure we go to bed by 10:00p.m. But then something happens. As the weeks go by, these new habits start slipping. We miss a day, then a week, then another. Soon enough, we're back to square one. Why is it so hard to make lasting changes to our day-to-day life?

"The only way to make sense out of change is to plunge into it, move with it, and join the dance." – Alan Watts

What's more important than habits?

Nothing. Habits form about 45% of your total behaviour, according to a Duke University study. Not only that, but they are behaviours that you repeat frequently, which compounds their significance in your life. Habits are your foundation, and if this foundation is weak, you won't be happy with the way you live.

"We are what we repeatedly do. Excellence, then, is not an act, but a habit."
—Aristotle

Do you know that feeling of being on autopilot? Think about your morning showers or brushing your teeth—you hardly need to think about what you are doing at all. Why? Because we've turned these necessary daily activities into habits; they become things we've done so often that we can do them automatically. Habits are something we don't have to make decisions about. They are pre-programmed into our daily life. Now, imagine what will happen if you successfully turn activities like eating healthier and working out into habits? You will be getting your healthy weight on autopilot mode! Isn't that amazing.

CARROT TRICK

Your subconscious mind drives your behaviors.

This is one of the tools to shift your mind, helping to change your lifestyle habits to healthy ones. This technique will assist to stay away from certain foods that you should avoid instantly. I call this technique the Carrot Trick.

What if a carrot tasted like chocolate? What if ice cream tasted disgusting and no longer appealed to you? What if going to run felt better than going to the pub? How easy would it be to be fit and healthy?

Ice cream is delicious, right? How can it possibly become unappealing? The truth is, right now, the pros of ice cream just outweigh the cons in your mind. So, you have to create the cons: think about that fatty aftertaste it leaves in your mouth. See that fatty aftertaste as a visible, irremovable film that sticks like glue to your mouth. Picture the cold, hard sugars rotting away at your teeth until they become painful and brown. Visualize the fat globules seeping through your insides, oozing their way through your blood vessels and adding themselves into heaving, pale-yellow piles of fat under your skin. Imagine the sound of all the saturated animal fats congealing into sickly putty and clogging up your arteries. How do you imagine that processed fat smells once it's stripped of its artificial flavors and sugars? **(These are powerful statements my clients love the most because they become inked into their mind; whenever they crave junk food, they automatically imagine fat globules seeping through their body.)**

How does that ice cream sound now?

Listen to that paragraph again if you need to. The more vividly you imagine these things, the better they will work. For added effect, put a plate of ice cream in front of you. Take one spoonful, put in your mouth and start to replay that paragraph. Focus on the negative aspects of the food, and they will soon outweigh the positive aspects. The results are that you won't want to buy more ice cream the next time you're at the supermarket.

The same goes for any food you like (but probably shouldn't eat), and the reverse goes for the food you don't like to eat (but probably should).

Let's take carrots, for example. Carrots are great because they actually require more calories to break down and process than they contain. Think about that, every fresh, crisp piece of carrot you bite and chew goes into your body and melts down fat. Not directly, of course, but for the purpose of this technique, let's pretend it does. In reality, your fat deposits are broken down by your body to gain energy for the processing of the carrot.

What is your favourite aspect of a carrot? If you hate the taste, then use a different vegetable for this example, possibly a piece of lettuce or celery. Picture the carrot being nicely broken down and literally turning old fat deposits into pure water. Concentrate on the taste. Say words like yummy and delicious, and really mean them. Act like it is the most delicious piece of food you have eaten in your entire life. Tell other people how great it tastes. Even if you don't quite believe it yourself, put on the performance of a lifetime. Your body will react by genuinely starting to like the carrot. This is the exact method I used on seaweed, which I used to hate but now enjoy. The more times you put on this act, and the more emotion you put behind your act, the faster this will work.

This tool works by tricking your brain into reconfiguring its reaction to certain foods. You are literally telling your brain that it is wrong; it's giving wrong signals. Your brain will react by correcting these problems in your favour. While there are millions of other things going on in your brain, these are the points we're interested in. This will not automatically and permanently change your perception of carrots.

You've only built one new pathway, compared to all the other thousands of times you've eaten ice cream and reacted naturally. Therefore, the more times you repeat this act, the stronger the effect will be and the easier and more natural the response will become. Eventually, you will develop a genuine taste for the carrot. I have always liked carrots, but since I used this technique on capsicum, I now consider them a delicious treat.

Use this mindset tool to work on your mind, and your mind will work on your body. But of course, I don't mean you can just lay on your bed and wonders will happen. You need to remind yourself that achieving your healthy weight is not so difficult. You just need to be consistent and focused. Focus on it, and consistently move toward it.

To prefer exercise or energy-consuming activities over sedentary activities, you need to rewire your brain a little bit. When you think, "Should I go exercise?" what is the first thing you picture? You picture yourself doing the exercise in question, and asking yourself how you would feel doing that. The answer is probably, "I'd feel tired. I'd need to put in a lot of effort and energy. It seems a bit too much like hard work."

No! Your brain doesn't tell YOU how to think! YOU tell your BRAIN how to think!

Now think, "Should I go exercise?" and immediately picture yourself having achieved a specific goal. If you don't have a goal, set one now.

Imagine you are looking at a YouTube clip of yourself in the future, the very moment you achieve that goal. Click on "play video" and see the screen displaying your future self-completing that goal for the first time. Close up on your face and see your expression as you achieve that goal. Listen to your breathing and see the sense of achievement spread across your face. Now step into the video and click "replay." Act it out in your mind – how does it feel?

How tempting does that exercise sound now?

You can perform the carrot trick to increase enjoyment during exercise.

When you're running up that steep hill or lifting that heavy weight, what are you thinking? Probably some sort of profanity-infused monologue regarding the unpleasantness of the situation. Why? There is no point.

Enjoy the feeling of the blood coursing through your body! How alive do you feel? Your body is operating on a large scale. This is the kind of thing kept billions of your evolutionary ancestors alive! Feel the rush of blood, the spirited tempo of your heart, and enjoy it! If you make this your focus and act it out, those endorphins come flooding in.

If you don't exercise regularly, I highly recommend trying it out. It doesn't have to be strenuous. Exercise shouldn't be too uncomfortable anyway, and I believe you should start as you mean to go on. If you start too hard, too fast, you can become overwhelmed and lose motivation. Music can help motivate you while you exercise too. If you are serious about being fit and healthy, exercise regularly and concentrate on the parts you do enjoy.

Motivation and Willpower Alone Don't Guarantee Success

The reason people fail to change their bad habits, and fail to instil new habits, is because they try to do too much at once. In simplest terms, if your new habit requires more willpower than you can muster, you will fail. If your new habit requires less willpower than you can muster, you will succeed.

"Good habits can make rational sense, but if they conflict with your identity, you will fail to put them into action." —James Clear

When we try to do something like lose 50 pounds or get in top physical condition, we're usually very excited for a couple days or weeks. We're highly motivated to eat healthy and be more active. Yet almost anyone who has attempted to change knows that sometime in those first weeks, motivation starts to wane.

The reason we lose motivation isn't a mystery. It's biological. And it's actually a positive sign! It means the behavior of eating healthy and being more active is transitioning to being controlled by the subconscious brain. In other words, a weak habit is forming. But right around this time is when most of us give up. We're not feeling that burst of enthusiasm anymore, so when it's gone, we'll stop doing the behavior that's just about to become a habit. It's too bad because the best way to find motivation is to take action!

Carrot Trick to Build Good Eating Habits / Exercise Habits

1. Identified any food you like (but probably shouldn't eat), and the reverse goes for the food you don't like to eat (but probably should).

2. Concrete on the cons for the food that you shouldn't eat, or concrete on the pros for the food you should eat.

3. Repeat it until it becomes your habit.

TINY HABITS

Back in 2009, PsyBlog examined the topic for a blog entry that looked at what the research tells us about how long it takes to form a new habit. Here's what they had to say:

"Although the average was 66 days, there was marked variation in how long habits took to form, anywhere from 18 days up to 254 days in the habits examined in this study. As you'd imagine, drinking a daily glass of water became automatic very quickly but doing 50 sit-ups before breakfast required more dedication (above, dotted lines). The researchers also noted that:

●Missing a single day did not reduce the chance of forming a habit.
●A sub-group took much longer than the others to form their habits, perhaps suggesting some people are 'habit-resistant.'
●Other types of habits may well take much longer."

Rome wasn't built in a day. You should take small and steady baby steps toward changing your behaviour.

Tiny Habits: The Small Changes That Change Everything by BJ, Ph.D., is an excellent guide to creating new habits, including weight loss habits. Dr. Fogg, a leading behavior change expert at Stanford University, presents behavior change in simple, practical steps based on his 20 years of research.

Dr. Fogg's model of behavior change explains that behaviors only happen when three key elements—motivation, ability, and a prompt—occur at the same time. B=MAP is an easy way to remember this; it is represented in the graph below.

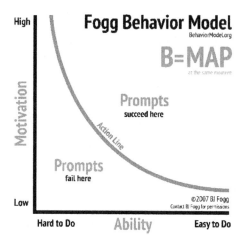

Fogg Behavior Model: Reprinted with approved license from DR BJ Fogg.

Motivation: Dr. Fogg explains that while some degree of motivation is needed, motivation can vary from day-to-day. We can't rely on motivation alone to build a habit.

Ability: Obviously, a behavior that takes a high level of ability or effort is less likely to happen. You may be very motivated to run a marathon, but your current lack of ability (never having run even 5 kilometers for 5 years) would make this behavior difficult (actually impossible).

A behavior goal that requires less ability (a tiny habit) is always doable, even when YOUR motivation is low. I may not be very motivated to go for 10 kilometers run when it is super-hot outside, but I can do 5 kilometers on the treadmill with my air-conditioning on.

Prompt: Dr. Fogg notes that a prompt is crucial. A successful habit is built by linking the new behavior to an existing behavior. He gives a quirky, yet effective, personal example of committing to doing two push-ups (behavior) after using the restroom (prompt). It apparently worked, as he reported a 20-pound weight loss after building on this habit!

Dr. Fogg provides this simple outline for creating tiny habits:

After I (prompt), I will (behavior).

Example: After I pee, I will do 2 push-ups.

"After I (normal routine), I will (new habit)."

We can apply this simple outline for your physical, intellectual, emotional, and spiritual health.

For instance, a simple morning routine:

After I wake up in the morning, I will drink water to nourish my body.
After I read the Bible, I will go for a 10-minute morning walk.
After I run, I will do breathing meditation for 5 minutes.
After I shower, I will read 5 pages of a book (by your own interest).
After I read, I will make my own healthy breakfast.
After I eat breakfast, I will take my supplements.

"People change best by feeling good, not by feeling bad." - BJ Fogg

Creating tiny habits is a perfect way to kickstart a new habit and keep it and transform it into a new behavior that becomes ingrained in your life. One small step of change can create massive impact. Therefore, we'll do it by changing your habits. Get lean, strong and confident starting from the inside out and creating long-lasting results.

Three Steps to Kick Start New Habits

1. Identify a new habit that is align with your health goal.

2. Using the outline: After I (normal routine), I will (new habit)."

3.   Test   it   and   restore   it.

MAGIC HABITS FOR A FLAT TUMMY

You may not need this, so treat it as a bonus.

HABIT #1. Contract the core and maintain great posture throughout the day.

It really comes down to just that. Squeeze the rectus abdominis all day long. Yes, I'm talking about standing up tall and trying to pull your belly button through to your spine.

The action of contracting activates your core muscles and helps you to maintain good posture.

Practicing good posture throughout the day is really going to give you a flat stomach.

Everyone can have a flat stomach, and that's where posture comes into play. If you stand up and try it right now, you'll notice that you instantly feel taller. Your shoulders will relax and you will immediately appear to have a smaller tummy.

Now, I'm not suggesting that you walk around all day sucking in your tummy. But if you, do it at regular intervals throughout the day while seated or standing, you will be strengthening your important core muscles.

Try to do 3 sets of 10-second holds. It's important that you practice contracting your abs while breathing.

It will take practice, but it is not wise to hold your breath while contracting your muscles.

Even when I'm driving, I'll sit up straight and pull my stomach in. It can be more effective than five minutes of abs, because you're constantly activating those muscles.

HABIT #2. Seated leg pull-ins.

Sit on the front edge of your chair with your legs together and bent at the knees, feet flat on the floor, back straight, and your shoulders back and relaxed. For more intense effect, lean back 45 degrees. Hold the seat of your chair on either side of your thighs, engage your abs, and, while still leaning back, slowly draw your knees in toward your chest.

You can do this movement whenever and wherever you want, be it at home, in the office or in the cinema. Moving your body helps to destress, relax, and improve circulation in your body. This is essential if you spend most of your time sitting in the same position all day. The human body is made to move. After all, doctors say any amount of exercise helps, and the benefits are cumulative

Worksheet: Creatures of Habits

What do you want to change? Or do differently?

_____

Tiny Habits recipe: (Start with 3 tiny habits and slowly increase more.)

After I......................., I will...........................

After I......................., I will...........................

After I......................., I will...........................

Review what have you achieved in one week, one month and one year.

_____

Suggested Readings:
BJ Fogg, Tiny Habits

CHAPTER 4

BUILD YOUR SHE SHED

Sheryl builds a she shed by the seashore'
The she shed is built with seashells.
Sheryl sits in seashell she shed,
She she'ier seashell she shed.

MY SHE SHED

If you have never heard about she shed, it's simply a private area for yourself to do your personal things. It's all about you.

Let me tell you little about my she shed.

My house has 4 bedrooms and 2 storerooms. The master room is for me and my husband; the other 2 bedrooms were previously occupied by my sisters and brother but they got their own houses so it's now turned into visitor rooms because my parents and my siblings visit us occasionally. Another room is more like a laundry room for us to hang wet clothes.

Eventually, I began to treat the living room as my she shed because I spend most of my time there and my working table is a big glass table. My husband has his home office upstairs.

It started simply because I needed a spacious place to practice morning yoga and meditation. I practice morning yoga and do my home workout and indoor biking here. I write in my daily journal and I started writing this book here. In my shed, I daydream, I sit back and reassess my day and where I am in my life.

I'm lucky enough to have a spacious living room to myself. The best is to have a whole room, but this might not be possible for everyone. It's perfectly fine if your she shed is nothing more than a corner of a room somewhere – a section, wall, table, garage space, something that is just for you. After all, it is all about you. If you love art, crafts or any projects that you have, put them nicely in one place. There should be a spot where you can sit, work, lie or meditate.

I'm not a fan of art or crafts. I keep my home workout "toys" in one of the living room corners. I also put my yoga mat there. Usually after yoga, I do a short meditation. Another corner with a glass top table is for me to work and write.

This she shed could be initially a spot for you to have some "me time" with your hobbies. As time passes, your hobbies also grow. One day, they could potentially turn into "passion projects." That's the power of manifestation.

DO JUST 1 THING

People spend 46.9 percent of their waking hours thinking about something other than what they're doing, and this mind-wandering typically makes them unhappy.
Research by psychologists Matthew A. Killingsworth and Daniel T. Gilbert of Harvard University is described in the journal Science.
"A human mind is a wandering mind, and a wandering mind is an unhappy mind," Killingsworth and Gilbert write. "The ability to think about what is not happening is a cognitive achievement that comes at an emotional cost."
When you try to do everything, you do nothing. To avoid doing nothing, we must focus in the moment, which requires choice, clarity, and commitment. Saying "I'm going to focus" is not enough.

You don't need pen and paper. You don't need anything except to keep three steps in mind. Mentally running through these steps at any time will have you focused in seconds.

So, how do you focus your mind instantly? It's simple: choose, clarify, and commit!

Choose ONE Objective
Don't say, "I'm going to focus."
Do ask, "What single thing am I going to focus on?"

This question will bring you to consider objectives. When you select one objective from a quick calculation of your situation and your most important tasks, THEN you can say, "I am going to focus on meditating!"

Take the pressure off yourself for choosing the very best task (perfectionism). What you choose matters less than you think. It's better to be focused on one good task than to be distracted with several potentially great tasks.

TUNE UP YOUR BRAIN WITH MEDITATION

In 1995, a study that was published in the Journal of Hypertension was conducted on 127 African Americans with very high, difficult to control blood pressure. The patients that were randomized to the meditation group were taught transcendental meditation. They were given a mantra, and they practiced meditation for 20 minutes twice a day. These individuals were able to drop their systolic blood pressure by 10.7 millimeters of mercury.

Meditation is the skillful, sustained, applied use of attention. The attention can be on your breath—breathing in and breathing out—or it can be on a word, but regardless of what you choose to focus on, your attention is focused. If you are new to meditation, you will find that your mind jumps around from thought to thought. It takes practice to control your mind.

When people begin to meditate, there is a reduction in addictive behaviors, such as cigarette smoking and alcohol use. We are just starting to understand the biochemistry of the brain, which might explain these effects, through functional MRI imaging.

A meditation practice may be formal or informal. The two most common forms of formal meditation that are used in health care are mindfulness-based stress reduction, which comes out of the Buddhist tradition, and transcendental meditation, which comes out of the Vedic tradition.

Research also shows that people who learn to meditate have a statistically significant reduction in anxiety. They feel less stressed, less anxious, and less worried. Transcendental meditation has even been shown to decrease insulin resistance.

Meditation can also be performed as an informal practice. You can informally practice meditation at any time any day. Whenever you get a free moment, take five longer, deeper breaths—five seconds in and five seconds out.

POWER OF GRATITUDE

While working on your body muscles, please do not forget your gratitude muscles.

"As we express our gratitude, we must never forget that the highest appreciation is not to utter words, but to live by them." – John F. Kennedy

There are many benefits to being grateful. Gratitude is good for your psychological well-being, your relationships, and possibly even your physical health. But the truth is that some people have more grateful dispositions than others. For some of us, gratitude just doesn't come as easy.

I have this habit, every day before I sleep, I will spend 5 minutes writing down my "gratitude list" of the day.

In a study published in the Journal of Personality and Social Psychology, it was found that individuals who counted their blessings on a frequent basis were more likely to be happy than individuals who didn't. This shows that creating a "gratitude list" can be a very useful tool in improving our happiness and well-being.

We often forget gratitude. There is so much to be grateful for, but we forget how precious it is to be alive. Remember to be grateful for your next breath.

To kick off this, you may consider doing it via the traditional way by having a booklet or journal, or use an environmentally friendly way by creating a Word document and typing the first 5 things that come into your mind that you are grateful for. Take a moment to reflect on each of the things on your list and why you are grateful for them.

Worksheet: Build Your She Shed

When I'm alone, I feel...

_____

While reading this chapter, I...

_____

If I were to compare my life with other people, my life is...

_____

CHAPTER 5

CONNECTING TO MOTHER NATURE

Take a walk in nature
Smell the wild air
Listen to birds chirping
Relax your soul

NATURE BATHING

Just a walk in the woods or a stroll by the beach on a sunny morning can awaken the innermost feelings of happiness and peace, and environmental psychology has gone a long way in proving this fact (Bell, Greene, Fisher, & Baum, 1996).

Our affinity toward nature is genetic and deep-rooted in evolution. Now pause and think about this: when you are planning for a vacation and in the midst of searching for the accommodations, did you realize that you naturally prefer to book accommodations that have sea views if you are going to a beach, or garden views? Why do patients who get a natural view from their hospital bed recover sooner than others? Or why does it happen that when stress takes a toll on our mind, we crave for time to figure out things faster in nature?

"One touch of nature makes the whole world kin." – William Shakespeare

I love to move on nature trails. I'm not a podium runner, at least not yet. I enjoy the scenery and seeing the flowers and the mountains, the water — just to move on technical terrain. When you hike you get to be in the beauty of nature. It's so much more pleasant. You get immersed in it, and you don't think about the elevation so much. Nature improves your psychological well-being.

•Nature helps with emotional regulation and improves memory functions. A study on the cognitive benefits of nature found that subjects who took a nature walk did better on a memory test than the subjects who walked down urban streets (Berman, Jonides, & Kaplan, 2008).
•A study at the University of Kansas found that spending more time outdoors and less time with electronic devices can increase problem-solving skills and improve creative abilities (Atchley, Strayer, & Atchley, 2012).
•Recent investigations reveal that being outdoor reduces stress by lowering the stress hormone cortisol (Gidlow, Randall, Gillman, Smith, & Jones, 2016).
•Nature walks benefit people suffering from depression. Studies show that people suffering from mild to major depressive disorders showed significant mood upliftment when exposed to nature. Not only that, but they also felt more motivated and energized to recover and get back to normalcy (Berman et al., 2012).

When I need a reset, the first thing that pops up in my mind is to take a walk in the community forest. I visit my dad's farm occasionally whenever I'm back at my parent's home, because my dad's farm is not as shady as the forest, and I was born with freckles. In order to reduce the freckles, I try my best to keep myself away from the hot sun. I like beach as much as I love the forest. You will be surprised to find out that my first bachelor's degree was in forestry. During those three years, I spent 50% of my time in Mother Nature doing fieldwork.

I try to get a dose of nature at least two times a week, with my pet, Hopee (a mix-breed dog that I adopted). A slow walk in the forest is like a moving meditation for me. I open every one of my senses to the trees and the land surrounding me, and I pay attention to grasshoppers and crickets in the grass as they make their "song" by rubbing legs and/or wings together and the expansive sky above me. These are familiar sensations: the crunch of leaves beneath boots, the beauty of a field of wildflowers. Fallen trees, brambles, rocks, and dead leaves make up the ground. The forest (tropical rainforests encompass between 59% to 70% of Malaysia's total land area) is swarming with animals and insects, so you hear a concert of humming, thrumming, buzzing and chirping. Howler monkeys and birds make some of the loudest rainforest sounds.

Of course, it's impossible to really imagine what it's like in the forest if you have never visited one. But reading about it and trying to connect it to real experiences can make it feel less like an abstract place. It's much easier to care about a place that you've been before, whether in real life or in your imagination. I highly recommend visiting a community forest near you at least once in your lifetime, and I'm 100% sure you will fall in love with nature.

You will also discover the friendliness, kindness, joy and peace of humans in the forest. Greet people you meet. This makes sure they know you are there and is polite. A simple "Howdy" or "Have a nice day" is fine. Always acknowledge your fellow hikers. Such basic gestures of friendliness distinguish your average wilderness encounter from its big city equivalent. Some see this as hiking etiquette, but I interpret these differently. When you open up to nature, you are away from stress and despair, you become calmer, you stop comparing yourselves to others, and you see things in neutral and without prejudgment; therefore, you become friendlier and you pay more attention to people and greet them with a happy mood.

When you connect to nature more, naturally you will start to appreciate the fresh air and clean water that you are enjoying every second. Open up to nature as part of your journey to being healthy from the inside out.

Tip #1: Find Nature Wherever You Are

We are surrounded by nature. Even if you stay in the city where nature can be limited, there's still places like community gardens and local parks to explore. Nowadays, most of the developers understand the needs of individuals and families who appreciate outdoor activities or nature; this sparks the ideas of green building, green environment and being eco-friendly. Each of the residential has unique selling theme, for instance, a spectacular treetop views of the green lung, a jogging track within the development, an urban park for the community and so on.

Try your best to look out for the unexpected wherever you can, in whatever way is meaningful for you. It could even be changes in the weather or birdsong outside your window.

Tip #2: Connect to Nature Using All Your Senses

Whether you are hiking, running or just relaxing in the garden or forest, open up your senses and be mindful with your natural surroundings, gazing upon green colors and lush forest landscapes, listening out for birds chirping, smelling the flowers, touching the rough bark of old trees, tasting the wild fruits.

In addition, using all your senses in the nature can give a real boost to your mental health.

Tip #3: Get in Nature

Instead of window shopping, or watching a movie at the cinema, get yourself out in nature. Spend a few hours during the weekends with your family or buddies, enjoying a picnic outing in green spaces like gardens or community forests. Expose yourself to sunshine.

Worksheet: Connecting to Mother Nature

List three places within 30 minutes' drive from your home where you can get connected to nature today.

_____

List three natural wonders within a 5-hour drive from your home where you can get connected to nature during the weekends.

_____

List three places anywhere in the world that would be your dream escape from civilization.

_____

CHAPTER 6

SLEEP MORE, STRESS LESS

It's not the stressful situation that kill you;
It's how you deal with stress that affects your health.
Find your inner peace, and
Prioritize your health.

Stress is our body's response to pressure. In life, different situations or events can cause stress, especially when we experience something new, unexpected or threatening to our sense of self, or when we feel we have little or no control over a situation.

Human being deals with stress differently. The ability to cope can depend on genetics, early life events, personality and social and economic circumstances.

As your body perceives stress, your adrenal glands make and release the hormone cortisol into your bloodstream. Also called the "stress hormone," cortisol causes an increase in your heart rate and blood pressure. It's the natural "flight or fight" response that has kept humans alive for thousands of years.

When you wake up in the morning or exercise, your body releases normal levels of cortisol. The normal levels can help regulate your blood pressure and blood sugar levels and even strengthen your heart muscle. The hormone can heighten memory, increase your immune system and lower sensitivity to pain in small doses.

The best remedies to relieve STRESS:
[S]pend time with family and friends
[T]houghtful (Mindfulness)
[R]educe caffein intake
[E]xercise
[S]oothing music
[S]sex

GET A D.O.S.E OF HAPPINESS

When we boost the D.O.S.E. of happiness, it will decrease the spike up of stress hormones. The acronym of D.O.S.E. represents

Dopamine
Oxytocin
Serotonin
Endorphins

Dopamine

Dopamine is also known as the "reward hormone." This hormone is responsible for our motivation, concentration, pleasure, bliss, and euphoria.

Dopamine can be released when we are doing activities such as exercise, meditation, listening to music or doing something creative such as painting or drawing.

Since this is a "reward hormone," with every achievement along the path to meeting our goal, our body releases dopamine into our brains, creating a sense of pleasure. This chemical keeps us focused and motivated. We physically feel good when we're taking steps towards our goals. Break long-term goals into short-term goals, with multiple measurable steps. This approach sets up a regular reward system of dopamine-induced motivation.

Dopamine is produced from amino acids that can be obtained from foods that are rich in L-tyrosine like sesame seeds, soybeans, meat and poultry.

Oxytocin

Oxytocin is also known as the "love hormone" for its role in childbirth and breastfeeding. Females have been shown to have a higher level of oxytocin than males. Oxytocin has been linked to higher self-esteem, trust, optimism, and mastery and can help lower stress and blood pressure.

This "love hormone," oxytocin, is released during physical contact such as cuddling and often sexual activity. It is also linked to relationships, bonding, and empathy.

We can also boost oxytocin through physical touch such as massage and acupuncture.

Serotonin

Serotonin is a chemical in the brain that can affect our mood. Serotonin is the key hormone that stabilizes our mood, feelings of well-being, and happiness. Serotonin also helps with sleeping, eating, and digestion. It also helps reduce depression and regulates anxiety. Reduced levels of serotonin may be causing low mood.

Foods, including eggs, salmon and spinach, that contain essential amino acid known as tryptophan help boost serotonin naturally.

Endorphins

We have all heard of a "runner's high." Endorphins are what is responsible for the euphoric feelings experienced after exercise. They can help to reduce pain, increase focus, and improve overall mood.

In addition to physical activity, endorphins can be released through laughter, sunshine, aromatherapy, and a healthy diet.

Summary of Activities to Boost D.O.S.E. of Happiness

Dopamine	Oxytocin	Serotonin	Endorphins
Meditate	Physical touch	Exercise	Laughter
Long-term goals	Socialising	Cold shower	Fun
Foods rich in L-tyrosine (sesame seeds, soybeans, meat and poultry)	Massage	Meditate	Exercise / stretching
	Listening to music	Sunlight	Massage
		Foods rich in tryptophan (salmon, eggs, spinach)	Meditate
	Acupuncture		
Exercise regularly	Exercise		Eat dark chocolate
	Cold shower		Eat spicy food
Get involved in creative activities like writing, music or arts.	Meditate		

TURNING STRESS INTO STRENGTH

People tend to think that stress is all bad, but it doesn't have to be. Without stress, we might feel demotivated, and if we're pushing our life forward or achieving our goals, stress can never be avoided.

The only one underlying root cause behind stress is perception. Stress isn't the problem, perception is. Perception is the lens through which we interpret and make sense of the world around us. It's the unique blend of images we hold in our minds about ourselves, others, the past, present and future.

"The mind is its own place, and in itself can make a heaven of hell, a hell of heaven." – John Milton

Stress and anxiety are the by-products of a negative perception of reality. We've been conditioned from birth to feel inadequate, to seek external approval and to live in fear. That is a lens that sees the world as a dangerous place, and a mind that constantly imagines worst-case scenarios. The result is a stressful life.

In this perceived world, stress is unavoidable. This world is full of ongoing worry, change, and uncertainty. You have to get used to it. Altering your approach to stress can yield positive effects.

Ultimately, in order to live a stress-free life, you need to build the courage to let go of your conditioned perception of reality, focus only on what you can control in the present moment and let go of everything else.

Tip #1: Recognize the Stress

Being stressed is a mindset, which means you have a choice. When you choose to recognize and understand that how much stress you feel is directly correlated to the importance of the activity. The stress itself becomes an indicator of how much you care about the task you are about to do. You won't feel stress or worry if the activity doesn't matter to you. Once you understand worry as an indicator rather than a symptom of dysfunction or a cause for panic, you can react to it more rationally. Plus, most panics only last for few minutes.

Tip #2: Reframe the Stress

Once you've recognized the stress, adjust your mindset. Our brains work better in positivity rather than stress. When you are stressed or worried, your brain goes into "fight or flight" mode, which limits your ability to think. If you are positive and concerned, then your brain turns to "broaden and build" thinking, which allows you to process more possibilities. This mental shift will allow the feeling to be activating rather than paralyzing.

Tip #3: Focus on What You Can Control

Whatever you focus on, and put more energy into, you're going to get more of it and win your life. One of the most positive things you can do when faced with worry or anxiety is to remember what you can affect and what you can't. Many people spend time feeling bad about things they simply can't change. Take a pause, list out all your stresses by asking yourself two questions:

1. What is within my control?

2. What matters most to me and what can I do about it?

Within our control are our own opinions, attitudes, dreams, desires, and goals. We control how we spend our time, what books we consume, how productive we are, what we eat, the number of hours we choose to sleep, and who we choose to spend time with.

Outside our control sits everything else: the family you were born into, how life's events unfold, the weather, the economy, other people...

Trying to control or change what isn't within your control will only drain your energy and leave you in torment. What you can control is how you perceive a situation, how you react to it, and how you respond. This will begin to solve the stress and move you toward your goal.

TAKE THE SLEEP CHALLENGE

Sleep is a powerful stress reducer. Sleep is a necessary human function that allows our brains to recharge and our bodies to rest. When we do not sleep long or well enough, our bodies do not get the full benefits of sleep, such as muscle repair and memory consolidation. Sleep is so crucial that even slight sleep deprivation or poor sleep can affect memory, judgment and mood. Research has shown that most Americans would be happier, healthier and safer if they were to sleep an extra 60 to 90 minutes per night.

Taking time to relax and wind down before bed is important to sleeping well and eliminating the stress of the day. Studies show that the melatonin level begins to increase around 9 to 10 p.m., this is when your body is looking for rest. The higher the melatonin level, the easier you will fall asleep and the better quality of sleep you will have. So even nature wants you to sleep early.

But why do most of not feel sleepy at 10:00 p.m.? Well, that's because these blue lights from gadgets have a short wavelength that is known to interfere with our circadian rhythm by delaying the production of melatonin. So, switch off your gadgets, switch off the lights and go to sleep. The idea is not to stimulate the mind but to calm it down so that you can sleep early. YES, relaxing just before bed is beneficial. Relaxation is a natural sleep aide that helps you calm your mind to fall asleep. Relaxation also helps you fall asleep in a positive frame of mind, which can help to decrease nightmares. Relaxation can be done by reading a book, or listening to relaxing music or using essential oils or taking a warm shower or meditating. You may consider having these foods, which will help you sleep better and faster, like warm milk. My preference is lavender hot tea with saffron; this tea is caffeine-free.

Worksheet: Sleep More, Stress Less

What caused your stress (make a guess if you're unsure)?

_____

How did you act in response to the stress?

_____

What did you do to make yourself feel better?

_____

PART 2: HYBRID HIIT (EXERCISE YOURSELF THIN)

CHAPTER 7

WHERE YOUR MIND GOES, YOUR BODY FOLLOWS

PAIN IS MENTAL

"You can chain me, you can torture me, you can even destroy this body, but you will never imprison my mind." – Mahatma Gandhi

In a study, researchers wanted to find out whether people could actually use their minds to enhance or reduce pain. Study subjects endured thermal stimulation on their arm multiple times. During some of the tests, they were asked to mentally "increase" or "decrease" the pain intensity. To increase it, they were told to imagine that the heat was more painful than it was, and to focus on how unpleasant the pain was (they were even told to picture their skin being held up against a glowing hot metal or fire and to visualize their skin melting and sizzling (ouch!).) To mentally decrease pain, they were told to imagine that the heat was less painful and to focus on the sensation being pleasantly warm, like a blanket on a cold day.

Turns out, these strategies have a lot to do with the consequences of pain. Pain was intensified when participants mentally increased pain and was less severe when they cognitively decreased it, says study author Tor Wager, Ph.D.

But this isn't just a technique to be used if you ever happen to get poked with a hot metal rod (here's hoping that doesn't happen). You can actually use this technique to help make exercise feel more comfortable. If your feet start to get sore during a long marathon training run, for example, don't distract yourself from the pain; change the way you think about it. Acknowledge that it's a sign you're working hard, but that it's not going to hurt you. "You can focus on the suffering part or you can focus on it as a kind of sensory experience that isn't necessarily bad," says Wager. "Think of it just as an experience, knowing that the pain won't actually harm you and that it will pass."

If you get a small blister or hot spot on your foot but you know you have another five kilometers to go, remind yourself that this isn't something that will hurt you. You can decide that it's going to be a huge problem and dwell on it, or you can think of it as a sign that you're pushing your body to get physical results and try to use your mind to reduce the pain sensation.

Pain is impossible to ignore—as soon as we feel something hurt, we're wired to start thinking about it to prevent future injuries, explains performance psychologist Jonathan Fader, Ph.D., the director of mental conditioning for the New York Giants. And, sometimes, discomfort is indeed a sign you need to back off. But most of the time, with proper form and the appropriate exertion, exercise-induced pain is really just a sign of cardiovascular conditioning or of muscles breaking down and building back stronger, he adds.

Powering through that healthy discomfort isn't just the avenue to becoming fitter and faster—it also helps you understand your physical limits more accurately so it hurts a little less next time.

GET OUT OF YOUR COMFORT ZONE

Everyone has comfort zones. Everyone has a list of things that they feel fine doing without one second thought, and then the other list of things that you cannot pay them to do.

You are smart enough to know that in order to achieve your healthy weight, you cannot keep doing the same old things that you have been doing for years. Stepping out of your comfort zone is the next step. Don't freak out at the fact that there is a "new" you in front of you.

What can you change so that your actions will ultimately take you to your health goals?

After going over your day and activities, don't you realize that you were not doing enough and will never get to your health goals? It's up to you to change that. Look at the list of things you are doing daily and think of just one change you can make that will take you one step closer to your health goals. Doesn't that sound great?

What are you doing to jump out of your comfort zone?

Now that you know what you need to do, do you feel ready? If you answered yes to that, stepping out of your comfort zone should feel a little uncomfortable, but you cannot expand your zone of comfort if you do not reach outside of it and stretch it.

"As you move outside of your comfort zone, what was once the unknown and frightening becomes your new normal." – Robin S. Sharma

Our mind is the most powerful thing in the world, and it's also our biggest weapon in our quest to look and feel amazing. The key is to convince yourself you can handle it, and yes, you definitely can. Once you are convinced and step out of your comfort zone, you will start to feel comfortable in the discomfort zone, and you will be closer to achieving your healthy weight! You are the one who needs to push yourself to reach new levels. As your strength and fitness grow rapidly, your body and mind will change to accept amazing new levels of challenge; your comfort zone will become greater.

Kickstart with 1% better in each workout, and soon you'll be 10% better.

Push 1% harder if you are new to the exercise, and soon you'll be 10% stronger.

Increase 1% intensity of each workout, and soon you'll get 10% more results.

I hear you. You want to have good shape, so you are going to have to push past your comfort zone, all the time. I'm guessing what you really want is a lean, strong and confident body.

PAUSE-BUTTON MENTALITY

The magic bullet to "making a fresh start" does not exist. "I'll resume exercise after my vacation… once the baby is born…on January 1… on Monday." While this kind of "pause-button mentality" seems reasonable, it could be ruining your health and fitness.

For most of us, the thought process boils down to this: If I miss some workouts, I fail. I will be more likely to succeed if I take a break, just until I have the time to do it right. I think it's normal to want to do your best. To consider taking time to regroup and then resume when life feels easier.

Starting fresh after you lose your way is a really comforting thought. That's probably why New Year's resolutions are so popular, especially following the indulgence-fueled holiday season.

"Give me that cheesecake. I'll pick my diet back up on Monday!"

"If only you'd let me start over, I'd really nail it this time!"

I remember having lunch with a girlfriend who swore up and down that her low-carb diet plus daily running was the secret to staying in shape. I had to follow up with a painful question: "Well, why aren't you actually in shape?"

After a long pause, she said, "Uhh, I've had a hard time sticking with it. We just had our second child and I just switched jobs." She trailed off...

"But, once everything settles down, I'll get with the program and get in shape again! I guess I'm just on a little break."

This story illustrates the point perfectly.

Ask yourself this: "What will be different when you come back?"

The honest answer is nothing. Nothing will be different.

Life is just...happening. And it'll happen again in January, or after the baby is born, or at any other arbitrary point you pick.

And what then?

I hit "pause" when I decided to focus on academics and stopped being active and continued eating the same way as I did when I was a competitive athlete, which caused me to gain 10 kilograms.

Let's accept that life has no pause button. The key lesson here is that, like it or not, the game of life keeps going. There is no timeout. There's never going to be a moment when things are magically easier.

You can't escape work or personal and family demands. Nor can you escape the need for health and fitness in your life.

Here's a thought experiment:

What if you tried to hit pause in other areas of your life? Imagine you're up for a big customer for your business. For the next two weeks, all you want to do is focus on an upcoming business proposal and presentation, and closing the deals.

Trouble is, you've got two young children at home who tend to grasp onto your legs and demand your full attention. Are you going to say to your spouse that you are just going to press pause on being a parent for the next two weeks?

You can't really press pause, and you definitely can't hit reset on being a parent or spouse. (You've thought about it, though. I know you have.) Just like you can't stop hustling for your living or dream life.

Life is just like a roller coaster. It has ups and downs. Sometimes we're superstars. Most of the time, we just do our best. We muddle through. We keep going.

So why do we expect it to be any different with exercise or fitness?

If you keep pressing pause, your progress will look like this:

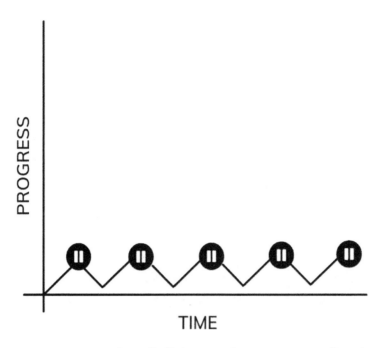

Or, worse yet, you end up flatlining, stuck on a never-ending (maybe eternal) pause.

The point is to keep going. Sometimes awkwardly or sometimes incompetently. But keep going nonetheless. Do not aim for perfection.

Fitness in the context of real human life is just like the rest of life.

We're all just doing the best we can in challenging, complicated circumstances. We are all living messy, imperfect lives. We are all human. If we can just keep moving forward, no matter what happens, no pause buttons, no do-overs, we win the game.

There are lots of incredible things about us humans, and one of the most fascinating things is our ability to observe what is going on in our mind. There is no other species that can do that. Not only can we know what is going on in our mind, but we can step back from it and observe

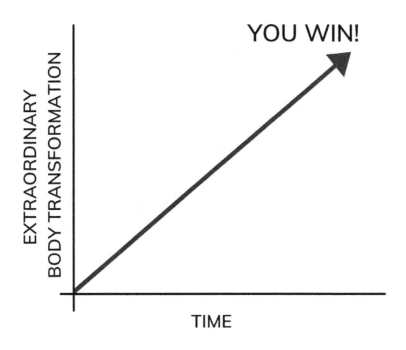

CHAPTER 8

MAGIC OF MANTRA – MIND OVER BODY

"Never give up what you want most for what you want today." –Neal A. Maxwell

I use mantras to keep myself motivated and to keep myself focused. If you've ever told yourself "You can do this" during certain important events, that's a mantra, too.

Mantras can do a lot of things, but the primary thing they can do is help you focus whenever you are uncertain of what the next right move might be. Mantras are the "magic bombs" of success; you can drop them right into your problem and, boom, the trouble goes away.

THE NEUROGICAL EFFECTS OF MANTRA ON YOUR BRAIN

One pilot study of mantra meditation with veterans found that a 5-week program significantly reduced symptoms of stress and anxiety and improved feelings of spirituality and well-being. The mantra meditation involves the repetition of certain words or phrases either out loud or silently.

Neuroscientists, equipped with advanced brain-imaging tools, are beginning to quantify and confirm some of the health benefits of this ancient practice, such as its ability to help free your mind of background chatter and calm your nervous system. In one study recently published in the Journal of Cognitive Enhancement, researchers from Linköping University, in Sweden, measured activity in a region of the brain called the default mode network—the area that's active during self-reflection and mind wandering—to determine how practicing mantra meditation affects the brain. From a mental health perspective, an overactive default mode network can mean that the brain is distracted, not calmed or centered.

We've long known that practicing asana, meditation, mantra, and mindfulness can improve health and happiness. Now, scientists are even uncovering how these practices can help prevent memory loss and delay the onset of more serious and scary cognitive impairments that often come with aging.

I also remember reading an article in Yoga Journal. Michael Trainer, a social entrepreneur, used classical music as meditation to heal his father's Alzheimer's disease. "I started to see that it was serving as an anchor in his mind, like a mantra; it had the power to bring him back to a calm place." I know this might not be acceptable by most people who are a "meat and potatoes" kind of person. It is always a challenge to implement new things to our lives. There's no harm in trying, so give it a try!

STOP WISHING, START DOING

Everyone has dreams. There is something that you would like to accomplish within a certain time frame. You wish to be healthier. This is good because it helps you to remain focused. However, even though this is a good thing, many people do not understand how to achieve it. Wishing only gives the desire of achieving your goals. Unless you act, you can be sure that the expected time will come and you will have done nothing. This is the reason why you have to stop wishing and start doing. This applies to all aspects of your life, be it in your physical, intellectual, emotional, and spiritual health.

In ultra-trail races, as in any other sports, there are times when you need to be thinking and times when you need to let go of active thinking and let your body react to situations as they unfold. Learning and trusting your body and letting go with your mind is an important skill. Whenever I feel as if I want to quit in the race, I will play this mantra in my head – "Finish like a pro." It helps me to push through. If I can do it, you can do it too!

Here are some of the mantras that work for me:

Fake it till you make it
What doesn't kill you makes you stronger
Finish like a pro
You can find an excuse or you can find a way
I'm doing this for me
Don't wish for it, work for it
If you are tired of starting over, stop giving up
Don't be afraid to be great
Nothing will work unless you do
Say yes to new adventures

Mantras are free! They have no side effects! They are simple and so easy!

There are millions of mantras out there, just googling "powerful mantras," "motivational mantras," and "mantra for success" will give you endless ideas to play with. But only you know what works for you. Choose what works for you.

CHAPTER 9

INTENSITY IS THE QUEEN

One sunny morning, I was walking in the morning park enjoying the fresh air. Suddenly, I heard this, "Don't kill yourself. I need you to be around when I get old," said a woman in her mid-thirties to the man in his early forties, both sitting on the bench with their comfortable sport outfits. The woman continued, "Not moving your body is equivalent to slow suicide." She was trying her best to convince the man, who I guess was her spouse or partner. She said this with full patience and love on her face.

I immediately linked to a research compilation by the World Health Organization, which concluded that 9% of all premature deaths are directly caused by inactivity. We are killing ourselves because we don't get up and move our bodies each and every day.

INTENSITY

Intensity is queen when it comes to fat loss. Intensity is a measure of how hard you are working. This can be measured by how you feel or quantified by heart rate, exercise speed, or incline.

A major misconception is the idea that low-intensity exercise is better for fat loss. Low-intensity exercise is often called the "fat burn zone." You can actually lose a whole lot of fat by exercising for far less time per day, but you must work out very hard. Although working out at a lower intensity will burn a higher percentage of calories from fat, when you work out at a higher intensity for the same amount of time, you burn far more calories.

Warming up, tuck jumps, full burpees, jumping jacks, weight training—all these were introduced to me when I was six. Those were body conditioning techniques that I had to practice each time before moving on with the actual badminton technique training. Then I had to run for 3 kilometers from the badminton studio back to home. That was an intense athlete training program for the competitive sports world.

"Sustained intensity equals ecstasy." – Wynton Marsalis

When it comes to healthy weight, you do not need to train like an elite athlete. Everyone's definition of intensity is a bit different. Running 5 kilometers for some runners is like warming up, but for someone who has never even run 1 kilometer in the past five years, this could be super intense.

"Practice makes progress." – Unknown

The point is to keep going. Sometimes awkwardly, sometimes incompetently, sometimes downright half-assed. But keep going nonetheless.

The intensity of your exercise depends on your personal goal!

If your personal goal is to have a toned body, in the aspect of exercise, you wouldn't have just focusing on low intensity workout. Nevertheless, other aspects of health, like nutrition, mindset, sleeping hours, stress management, water intake and supplements, are equally important.

HIIT

Personally, I do a lot of cardio because I'm an ultra-runner. But I know most people do not favour running due to a lot of reasons, such as time, knee pain, etc.

"Train and achieve fantastic and permanent results in the same amount of time."

Therefore, I did a study and tested it out myself for 12 weeks on the most effective workout, which is the high-intensity interval training and Tabata. Research shows that short HIIT workouts can be used to increase both aerobic and anaerobic fitness, promote fat loss, and even improve blood pressure, insulin sensitivity, and glucose regulation in a relatively short time.

If you need any convincing about why high-intensity exercise (HIE) is the key to reshaping your body, check out this study from the International Journal of Obesity. It shows the results of fifteen weeks of high-intensity exercise (HIE) versus steady-state exercise (SSE) and a control group that did no workout (CONT). The left shows the overall loss of pure fat up to 2.5 kilograms and 1.5 kilograms of abdominal fat. Those who did steady-state workouts actually gained a little bit of fat.

Weight loss is not fat loss. Weight loss refers to a decrease in your overall body weight from muscle, water, and fat losses. Fat loss refers to weight loss from fat, and it's a more specific and healthful goal than weight loss.

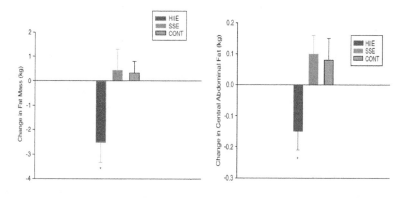

Chart 2
Source: Trapp EG, Chisholm DJ, Freund J, Boutcher SH. "The effects of high-intensity intermittent exercise training on fat loss and fasting insulin levels of young women." International Journal of Obesity. 2008;32(4):684-691.

HIIT versus Tabata

These two styles of training stem from the same branch. Both Tabata and HIIT are forms of interval training. Interval training is a form of cardiovascular exercise that aims to raise and lower your heart rate repeatedly, in order to boost your metabolism.

Tabata and HIIT also increase EPOC, which stands for excess post-exercise oxygen consumption. EPOC allows us to keep burning calories for up to 2 hours after exercise. This means that you'll burn more calories overall while improving your heart and lung health.

	Cardiovascular Fitness		Body Composition	
Author (Year)	ET	HIIT	ET	HIIT
Tabata et al. (1996)	9% increase	13% increase	NS	NS
Tremblay et al. (1994)	24% increase	20% increase	No change sum of six skinfolds	Significant decrease sum of six skinfolds
Trapp et al. (2008)	17% increase	21% increase	No change in percent body fat	Significant decrease in percent body fat
Helgerud et al. (2007)	5% increase	7.2% increase	No change in body mass	Significant decrease in body mass

ET indicates endurance training; HIIT, high-intensity interval training; NS, not studied.

Table 1
Source: ACSM's Health & Fitness Journal 18(5):17-24, September/October 2014.

Table 1 presents a number of HIIT studies and shows the changes in cardiorespiratory fitness and body composition. Within, and even across studies, the changes in V˙O2max are quite similar. Once again though, it is important to remember that the HIIT groups, like the subjects in the Tabata study, did substantially less exercise and expended fewer calories than the ET groups. Therefore, the contention that Tabata and HIIT could produce similar or even superior changes in fitness.

"Tabata, like HIIT, is an exercise format that alternates relatively brief periods of intense exercise, often called "effort" intervals, with periods of rest or less-intense exercise, known as "recovery" intervals. Tabata is one of the most popular forms of shorter HIIT workouts and was first popularized by Dr. Izumi Tabata. Dr. Tabata coupled 20 seconds of "supramaximal" anaerobic effort with just 10 seconds of recovery for 8 rounds, making the exercise session quite short. At just 4 minutes in duration, Tabata's research showed that this exercise protocol delivers impressive changes in fitness. Modified Tabata workouts that range between 4 and 20 minutes in duration can be less intense but still robust (i.e., 74% to 95% of max) such as Tabata-style circuits. Research shows that Tabata and HIIT produce similar changes in cardiovascular fitness, have the potential to improve body composition, and can even ameliorate risk factors such as insulin action in far less time compared with traditional, moderate-intensity, steady-state 30- to 40-minute cardio sessions. When implementing Tabata and Tabata-style HIIT workouts, trainers should determine the appropriateness of this intense type of interval training for a given client or group and select the volume, intensity, and specific exercise activities that best match the needs and capabilities of the participant(s)." Olson, Michele Ph.

REST DAY

"Rest is not idleness, and to lie sometimes on the grass under a tree on a summer's day, listening to the murmur of the water, or watching the clouds float across the sky, is by no means a waste of time." – John Lubbock

We're always told to stay active and get regular exercise. But more isn't always better.

Rest days are just as important as exercise. Taking regular breaks allows your body to recover and repair. It's a critical part of progress, regardless of your fitness level. Otherwise, skipping rest days can lead to overtraining or burnout.

If you're trying to lose weight, you should still have regular rest days.

Rest allows your muscles to rebuild and grow. And when you have more muscle, you'll burn more calories at rest. That's because muscle burns more energy than fat.

Additionally, when you feel refreshed, you'll be more likely to stick to your exercise routine.

The top three benefits of taking a rest day are: -

Tip #1: Allows time for recovery

Specifically, rest is essential for muscle growth. Exercise creates microscopic tears in your muscle tissue. But during rest, cells called fibroblasts repair it. This helps the tissue heal and grow, resulting in stronger muscles.

Also, your muscles store carbohydrates in the form of glycogen. During exercise, your body breaks down glycogen to fuel your workout. Rest gives your body time to replenish these energy stores before your next workout.

Tip #2: Prevents muscle fatigue

Rest is necessary for avoiding exercise-induced fatigue. Remember, exercise depletes your muscles' glycogen levels. If these stores aren't replaced, you'll experience muscle fatigue and soreness.

Plus, your muscles need glycogen to function, even when you're not working out. By getting adequate rest, you'll prevent fatigue by letting your glycogen stores refill.

Tip #3: Reduces risk of injury

Regular rest is essential for staying safe during exercise. When your body is overworked, you'll be more likely to fall out of form, drop a weight, or take a wrong step.

Overtraining also exposes your muscles to repetitive stress and strain. This increases the risk of overuse injuries, forcing you to take more rest days than planned.

In a study, researchers wanted to find out whether people could actually use their minds to enhance or reduce pain. Study subjects endured thermal stimulation on their arm multiple times. During some of the tests, they were asked to mentally "increase" or "decrease" the pain intensity. To increase it, they were told to imagine that the heat was more painful than it was, and to focus on how unpleasant the pain was (they were even told to picture their skin being held up against a glowing hot metal or fire and to visualize their skin melting and sizzling (ouch!).) To mentally decrease pain, they were told to imagine that the heat was less painful and to focus on the sensation being pleasantly warm, like a blanket on a cold day.

12-WEEK WORKOUT PLAN

Weekly Workout Schedule

This 12-week workout plan is results-proven by world-class athletes; it was tested on hundreds of men and women at all ages and sizes, and it ended up that the hundred people dropped pounds as well as sculpting their bodies.

There are in total seven workouts weekly. Each workout is designed to take around twenty to twenty-five minutes, except for long-circuit, which will take between thirty and forty minutes. If you really have a tight schedule, feel free to adjust it because you know better about your own schedule. What matters is seven workouts in a week!

Monday	Upper Body Workout (P.M.)
Tuesday	Cardio (A.M.) and Lower Body Workout (P.M.)
Wednesday	Cardio (A.M.) and Abs Workout (P.M.)
Thursday	Cardio Workout (A.M. or P.M.)
Friday	Rest
Saturday	Long Circuit Workout (A.M. or P.M.)
Sunday	Rest

AMRAP: As Many Reps As Possible. It means do as many repetitions of the exercise as you can within a period of time.

Equipment needed:

- Bench/ chair
- Jump rope
- Set of dumbbells (5 pounds or more)
- Mat
- Tabata timer (use your smartphone)

For exercise demonstrations, you can go to http://www.thinkandbethin.com/ to watch the video of me demonstrating each of the moves.

Are you getting excited to kick off?

I know you definitely are!

Get ready. Get set. Go! Go! Go!

Week #1 Workout

Cardio	
Cardio 1	
Warm-up:	Jog / run
20 min	
Cardio 2	
Warm-up:	Jog/ run
20 min	10 air squats
	10 walking lunges (5 each side)
Cardio 3	
Warm-up:	Jog / run
20 min	
Upper Body	
100 butt kickers	
100 jumping jacks	
100 jump ropes	
No rest	
5 rounds:	20 knee push-ups
	20 Superman
	20 jumping jacks
	20 straight leg triceps dips
Lower Body	
10 min AMRAP:	20 lunges (10 each side)
3 rounds	20 squats
	20 step- ups (10 each side)
	20 sumo squat kick (10 each side)
	1 min wall sits
Rest 1 min	
Repeat	
Abs	
3 rounds	
6 min:	1 min full plank
	1 min elbow plank
	Raised leg plank (30 sec each leg)
	Side plank (30 sec each side)
	1 min full plank
	1 min elbow plank

Rest 1 min	
	30 abs bikes (15 each side)
	30 ankle touches (15 each side)
	15 snap jumps
	30 easy mountain climbers (15 each side)
Repeat	

Long Circuit

3 rounds:	10 air squats
	10 incline push-ups
	10 planks to downward dog
	Rest 30 sec
Rest 1 min	
Run 8 min	
Rest 1 min	
10 min AMRAP:	10 no-push-up burpees
	20 step- ups (10 each side)
	15 snaps jump
Rest 1 min	
100 knee push-ups	

Week #2 Workout

Cardio	
Cardio 1	
Warm-up:	Jog/ run
20 min	
Cardio 2	
Warm-up:	Jog/ run
20 min	20 air squats
Cardio 3	
Warm-up:	Jog/ run
20 min	20 walking lunges (10 each side)
Upper Body	
15 min AMRAP:	10 inchworms
	20 no push-up burpees
	15 knee push-ups
Rest 1 min	
15 min AMRAP:	10 Superman
	20 straight leg triceps dips
	20 jumping jacks
Lower Body	
3 rounds	
10 min AMRAP:	20 lunges (10 each side)
	20 deep squats
	20 step-ups (10 each side)
	20 side-to-side squats (10 each side)
	2 min wall sits
Rest 1 min	
Repeat	
Abs	
3 rounds	
6 min:	1 min full plank
	1 min elbow plank
	Raised leg plank (30 sec each leg)
	Side plank (30 sec each side)
	1 min full plank
	1 min elbow plank
Rest 1 min	
	30 abs bikes (15 each side)

	30 ankle touches (15 each side)
	30 snap jumps
	30 easy mountain climbers (15 each side)
Repeat	

Long Circuit

3 rounds:	Butt kickers 30 sec
	Jumping jacks 30 sec
	Lunges 30 sec
	Rest 30 sec
Rest 2 min	
Run 5 min	
30 push-ups	
Run 5 min	
30 bench jumps	
Run 5 min	
30 squats with arms overhead	
Run 5 min	
30 sumo squat kick (15 each side)	

Week #3 Workout

Cardio	
Cardio 1	
Warm-up:	Jog/ run 5 min
4 rounds	Right-side shuffle 20 sec
	Left-side shuffle 20 sec
Cardio 2	
Warm-up:	Jog/ run
20 min	20 air squats
Cardio 3	
Warm-up:	Jog/ run
20 min	20 walking lunges (10 each side)

Upper Body
1 min squat jacks
1 min commandos
1 min side to side hops
1 min knee push-ups
Rest 1 min
Repeat the same moves for 30 sec each as fast as you can
Rest 1 min
1 min no push-ups burpees
1 min bent-leg triceps dips
1 min jumping jacks
1 min inchworm and push-up
Rest 1 min
Repeat the same moves for 30 sec each as fast as you can

Lower Body	
5 rounds:	1 min hop overs
	Rest 20 sec
	1 min lunges
	Rest 20 sec
	1 min squat jumps
	Rest 20 sec
	1 min alternating squat and kick
	Rest 20 sec

Abs	
3 rounds	
5 min AMRAP:	20 right-side plank hip dips

	20 left-side plank hip dips
	High knees 30 sec
Rest 1 min	
5 min AMRAP:	30 mason twists (15 each side)
	30 crossover toe touches (15 each side)
	20 feet-anchored sit-ups
Rest 1 min	
Repeat	
Long Circuit	
50 air squats	
Rest 2 min	
21-15-9	Dumbbell swings
	Bench jumps
	Squat jumps
	Dumbbell squat curls and presses
Rest 2 min	
50 no-push-up burpees	
Rest 2 min	
21-15-9	Push-ups
	Butterfly sit-ups
	Shoulder presses
	Curls and presses

Week #4 Workout

Cardio	
Cardio 1	
Warm-up:	Jog/ run
20 min	10 no-push-up burpees
Cardio 2	
Warm-up:	Jog/ run
20 min	1 min wall sit
21-15-9	
Cardio 3	
Warm-up:	Jog/ run
20 min	20 hop overs (10 each side)
Upper Body	
10 rounds	8 no push-ups burpees
	8 inchworms
	8 knee push-ups with elbow in
	8 bent-leg triceps dips
Rest 1 min	
Repeat	
Lower Body	
4 rounds:	30 air squats
	30 step-ups (15 each side)
	30 reverse lunges and knee lifts
	1 min bench toe taps
Rest 1 min	
Repeat	
Abs	
Tabata: Complete the full 4 min Tabata cycle for each move, then a 1 min rest period before you start the next move.	
5 rounds:	Butterfly sit-ups
	Plank
	Ab bikes
	Easy mountain climbers
Long Circuit	
Tabata: Complete the full 4 min Tabata cycle for each move, then a 1 min rest period before you start the next move.	

	Air squats
	Jumping jacks
	Hollow body hold
2 rounds:	100 hop overs
	50 lunges (25 each side)
	100 jump ropes
	50 knee push-ups
Rest 2 min	
3 rounds:	10 curls and presses
	10 reverse flies
	10 lateral raises

For those 4 min are intense, you can do this:

- **Push yourself as hard as you can for 20 seconds**
- **Rest for 10 seconds**
- **Complete 8 rounds (for a total of 4 min)**

Tabata Timer- simple (IOS apps)

Week #5 Workout

Cardio	
Cardio 1	
Warm-up:	Jog/ run
20 min	
Cardio 2	
Warm-up:	Jog/ run
20 min	
Cardio 3	
Warm-up:	Jog/ run
20 min	20 walking lunges (10 each side)
Upper Body	
50-40-30-20-10	Push-ups
	Straight-leg triceps dips
	Commandos
Lower Body	
9 min AMRAP:	20 jumping lunges (10 each side)
	20 weighted sumo squats
	20 step-ups and knee lifts (10 each side)
	10 squat jumps
Rest 1 min	
9 min AMRAP:	10 broad jumps
	20 step-ups (10 each side)
	20 weighted lunges (10 each side)
	10 tuck jumps
5 min	Wall sit and arms overhead 30 sec
	Rest 30 sec
Abs	
8 min AMRAP:	30 hip dips (15 each side)
	20 no-push-up burpees
	10 hollow rocks
Rest 1 min	
8 min AMRAP:	30 ab bikes (15 each side)
	20 mason twists (10 each side)
	10 straight-leg raises and hip lifts
Rest 1 min	
Tabata: full mountain climbers	

Long Circuit

500 m run

50 bench jumps

50 push-ups

Rest 3 min

500 m run

50 snap jumps

50 air squats

Rest 3 min

500 m run

50 mountain climbers (25 each side)

50 full burpees

Week #6 Workout

Cardio	
Cardio 1	
Warm-up:	Jog/ run
20 min	10 no-push-up burpees
Cardio 2	
Warm-up:	Jog/ run
20 min	
Cardio 3	
Warm-up:	Jog/ run
20 min	
Upper Body	
3 rounds:	Downward dog 30 sec
	5 reverse tabletop swings
	3 wall walks
Rest 1 min	
100 jump ropes / 5 Superman	
80 jump ropes / 10 Superman	
60 jump ropes / 15 Superman	
40 jump ropes / 20 Superman	
20 jump ropes / 25 Superman	
60 jump ropes / 15 Superman	
80 jump ropes / 10 Superman	
100 jump ropes / 5 Superman	
Rest 1 min	
Tabata push-up	
Lower Body	
Tabata: Rest 1 min between each movement	
	Air squats
	Hop overs
	In/out squat jumps
	Jump ropes
Abs	
3 Rounds:	
50 jump ropes	
50 full mountain climbers (25 each side)	
50 jump ropes	
50 mason twists (25 each side)	

50 jump ropes	
50 butterfly sit-ups	
50 jump ropes	
50 seated in/outs	
50 jump ropes	
50 snap jumps	
50 jump ropes	
50 hip dips (25 each side)	
Repeat	
Long Circuit	
50-40-30-20-10	Weighted overhead lunges
	Air squats
	Bent-knee sit-ups
Rest 3 min	
3 rounds:	30 hop overs (15 each side)
	15 burpees and tuck jumps
Rest 1 min	
Tabata: push-ups	

Week #7 Workout

Cardio	
Cardio 1	
Warm-up:	Jog/ run
20 min	10 butt kickers
	10 high knees
Cardio 2	
Warm-up:	Jog/ run
20 min	Walking lunge
Cardio 3	
Warm-up:	Jog/ run
20 min	
Upper Body	
4 rounds:	20 full burpees
	20 commandos (10 each side)
	20 dumbbell thrusters
	20 push-ups with elbows in
Lower Body	
10 tuck jumps	
20 squat jumps	
20 jumping lunges (15 each side)	
40 step-ups (20 each side)	
50 squat jumps	
10 tuck jumps	
Rest 3 min	
2 rounds:	50 weighted sumo squats
	50 weighted lunges (25 each side)
Abs	
6 rounds	10 Hollow rocks
	20 planks knee to elbow (10 each side)
	10 hollow rocks
	20 alternating twist sit-ups (10 each side)
	Rest 1 min
Long Circuit	

Run 10 min
Rest 3 min
25 bent-leg triceps dips / 25 push-ups
20 bent-leg triceps dips / 20 push-ups
15 bent-leg triceps dips / 15 push-ups
10 bent-leg triceps dips / 10 push-ups
10 bent-leg triceps dips / 10 push-ups
Rest 3 min
50 ab bikes (25 each side)/ 50 full mountain climbers (25 each side)
40 ab bikes / 40 full mountain climbers
30 ab bikes / 30 full mountain climbers
20 ab bikes / 20 full mountain climbers
10 ab bikes / 10 full mountain climbers
Rest 3 min
25 tuck jumps / 25 squat jumps
20 tuck jumps / 20 squat jumps
15 tuck jumps / 15 squat jumps
10 tuck jumps / 10 squat jumps
10 tuck jumps / 10 squat jumps

Week #8 Workout

Cardio	
Cardio 1	
Warm-up:	Jog/ run
25 min	10 butt kickers
	10 high knees
Cardio 2	
Warm-up:	Jog/ run
25 min	Squat jumps
Cardio 3	
Warm-up:	Jog/ run
25 min	

Upper Body	
3 Rounds	
6 min AMRAP	15 dumbbell squat curls and presses
	30 plank shoulder taps (15 each side)
	16 dumbbell press (8 each side)
	8 inchworms + push up with elbows in
Rest 1 min	
6 min AMRAP	15 decline push-ups
	15 full burpees
	15 reverse flies
	15 bent-legs triceps dips
Rest 1 min	
Repeat	

Lower Body	
3 Rounds	
Butt kickers + arms up 1 min	
Yogi squats 30 sec	
Jumping jacks 1 min	
Yogi squats 30 sec	
High knees 1 min	
Yogi squats 30 sec	
Repeat	
15 min AMRAP	10 full burpees
	10 reverse lunges + knee hop (5 each side)
	10 sumo squat jumps with 2 sec holds at the bottom

Abs	
3 Rounds	
6 min AMRAP	15 roll back to stand
	15 plank in / outs + snap jumps
	15 tuck jumps
Rest 1 min	
6 min AMRAP	15 right-side sit-ups
	15 left-side sit-ups
	15 straight-leg raise + hip lift
Rest 1 min	
Repeat	

Long Circuit
100 jump ropes
90 air squats
80 lunges (40 each side)
70 butterfly sit-ups
60 push-ups with elbows in
50 step-ups (25 each side)
40 mason twist (20 each side)
30 dumbbell push press
20 burpees
10 broad jumps
20 burpees
30 dumbbell push press
40 mason twist (20 each side)
50 step-ups (25 each side)
60 push-ups with elbows in
70 butterfly sit-ups
80 lunges (40 each side)
90 air squats
100 jump ropes

Week #9 Workout

Cardio	
Cardio 1	
Warm-up:	Jog/ run
20 min	Right-side shuffle 30 sec
	Left-side shuffle 30 sec
Cardio 2	
Warm-up:	Jog/ run
20 min	15 air squats
	10 jumping lunges
Cardio 3	
Warm-up:	Jog/ run
20 min	
Upper Body	
3 Rounds	100 jump ropes
	3 wall walks
Rest 2 min	
15 min AMRAP	10-man makers
	20 dumbbell swings
Lower Body	
Tabata: Rest 1 min after each move	
	Jump ropes
	Squat jumps
	Jumping jacks
10 min AMRAP	30 side sumo squats + kicks (15 each side)
	30 weighted step-ups
	20 broad jumps
	20 weighted reverse lunges (10 each side)
Abs	
3 Rounds	20 alternating twist sit-ups (10 each side)
	Rest 30 sec
	Upright ab bikes 1 min
Rest 30 sec	
	Hip dips 1 min
Rest 30 sec	
	Double mountain climbers 1 min

Rest 30 sec	
	High knees 1 min
Rest 30 sec	

Long Circuit

Jumping lunges 1 min

Air squats 1 min

Squat jumps 1 min

Alternating side-step sumo squats 1 min

No push-ups burpees 1 min

Lunges 1 min

Repeat the same moves for 30 sec each as fast as you can

Rest 3 min

Abs bikes 1 min

Full mountain climbers 1 min

Butterfly sit-ups 1 min

L-sit toe touches 1 min

Hip dips 1 min

Crossover toe touches 1 min

Repeat the same moves for 30 sec each as fast as you can

Rest 3 min

Push-ups 1 min

Bent-leg triceps dips 1 min

Plank in/ outs 1 min

Full burpees 1 min

Snap jumps 1 min

Commandos 1 min

Repeat the same moves for 30 sec each as fast as you can

Week #10 Workout

Cardio	
Cardio 1	
Warm-up:	Jog/ run
20 min	

Cardio 2	
Warm-up:	Jog/ run
20 min	

Cardio 3	
Warm-up:	Jog/ run
20 min	20 Hop overs (10 each side)

Upper Body	
Tabata: Rest 1 min between movements	
	Push-ups
	Bent-leg triceps dips
	Jump ropes

Lower Body	
10 min AMRAP	15 burpee hop overs
	20 double-pulse squat jumps
	20 dumbbells back squats
	30 jumping lunges (15 each side)
Rest 2 min	
10 min AMRAP	15 burpee bench jumps
	30 reverse lunges + knee hops (15 each side)
	20 crossovers jump squats (10 each side)
	30 bench hops

Abs
10 burpee tuck jumps
20 Hollow rocks
30 alternating twist sit-ups (15 each side)
40 hip lifts
50 weighted mason twists (25 each side)

60 butterfly sit-ups
70 snap jumps
80 ab bikes (40 each side)
Plank hold 90 sec
100 alternating side squats + front kicks (50 each side)
Long Circuit
Run 1 mile
100 sit-ups
100 push-ups
100 air squats
100 dumbbell push press
Run 1 mile

Week #11 Workout

Cardio	
Cardio 1	
Warm-up:	Jog/ run
20 min	
Cardio 2	
Warm-up:	Jog/ run
20 min	10 tuck jumps
	10 air squats
Cardio 3	
Warm-up:	Jog/ run
20 min	
Upper Body	
2 Rounds	
7 min AMRAP	20 squat curls and presses
	20 full burpees
	20 reverse flies
Rest 1 min	
7 min AMRAP	20 bent-legs triceps dips
	20 lateral raises
	20 straight-legs triceps dips
Rest 1 min	
Repeat	
Lower Body	
5 min AMRAP	50 jump ropes
	25 air squats
Rest 1 min	
50 bench jumps	
50 jumping lunges (25 each side)	
50 hop overs (25 each side)	
50 dumbbell thrusters	
50 dumbbells back squats	
50 bench hops (25 each side)	
50 double mountain climbers	
Abs	
3 Rounds	50 high knees (25 each side)
	50 full mountain climbers (25 each side)

	50 butt kickers (25 each side)
	50 weighted mason twists (25 each side)
Rest 30 sec	
3 Rounds	20 tuck jumps
	20 alternating twist sit-ups (10 each side)
	20 snap jumps
	20 knee-ups
Rest 30 sec	
Long Circuit	
3 Rounds	60 jump ropes
	60 jumping jacks
	Yogi squat 60 sec
Rest 1 min	
21-15-9	Dumbbell thrusters
	Full burpees
Rest 5 min	
3 Rounds	30 push-ups with elbow in
	30 bent-legs triceps dips
	30 bench jumps
Rest 2 min	
Tabata: hollow body hold	

Week #12 Workout

Cardio	
Cardio 1	
Warm-up:	Jog/ run
20 min	
Cardio 2	
Warm-up:	Jog/ run
20 min	10 jumping lunges
	10 air squats
Cardio 3	
Warm-up:	Jog/ run
20 min	
Upper Body	
50 jumping jacks	
40 air squats	
30 snap jumps	
20 squat jumps	
10 push-ups	
Rest 2 min	
20 min AMRAP	5/5, 10/10. 15/15, 20/20, 25/25. Etc.
	Dumbbell thrusters
	Burpee hop overs
Lower Body	
2 Rounds	
6 min AMRAP	12 sumo squats
	24 squat toe taps (12 each side)
	12 hop overs (6 each side)
Rest 3 min	
6 min AMRAP	12 broad jumps
	12 dumbbell thrusters
	12 dumbbells back squats
Abs	
2 Rounds	20 Hollow rocks
	20 butterfly sit-ups
	20 L-sit toe touches
Tabata: full mountain climbers (25 each side)	
Rest 1 min	

2 Rounds	20 weighted mason twists (10 each side)
	20 upright ab bikes (10 each side)
	20 crossover toe touches (10 each side)
Tabata: plank knee to elbow	
Rest 1 min	
2 Rounds	20 right-side sit-ups
	20 left-side sit-ups
	20 hip lifts
Tabata: hollow body hold	
Long Circuit	
8 min AMRAP	200m run
	Rest 30 sec
Rest 4 min	
8 min AMRAP	12 Yogi squats
	12 straight-leg triceps dips
	12 decline push-ups
Rest 4 min	
8 min AMRAP	12 tuck jumps
	12 jumping lunges (6 each side)
	12 air squats
Rest 4 min	
8 min AMRAP	12 plank in/ outs + snap jumps
	12 bent-knee sit-ups
	12 weighted mason twists (6 each side)

For movements demonstrations, you can go to http://www.thinkandbethin.com/ to watch the video of me demonstrating each of the moves.

PART 3: SURVIVAL INSTINCT (LEARN YOUR WAY THIN)

CHAPTER 10

THE EATING INSTINCT

(Oxford dictionary: non-conscious, innate survival tendencies. The role of instincts driving social behaviour is so important that instincts deserve special attention and clarification, especially over definitions.)

Consuming food is an inherently basic survival instinct of all life forms; each one, small or big, needs water and food to survive. The entire biological web has survived and is recycled within the food chain. The instinct of eating or being fed is inborn; even a few-hours-old infant grabs his palm and takes it to the mouth. A normal, growing baby continues to grab just anything and takes it to the mouth thereby proving the universality of food intake for survival.

So how do you stop eating instinctly? This is the most magical part. An original food's taste will actually change in your mouth as your body's nourishment needs are met. For instance, honey or seaweed that at first tastes exquisite will become less and less delicious until it is actually painful to continue to eat. Really! The sensory experience changes even though the food remains the same. That's because the body is a most sophisticated signal-receiving and data-processing organism. It's perfectly designed to prevent overeating thanks to the taste change. Even if you are still hungry, you will not be able to eat more of a particular food as long as you are sensitive to your body's messages to stop. Why? It just won't taste good anymore unless you use condiments to mask and extend the flavor of this now non-nourishing edible.

This basic process is effortless and present in all human or animals. Essentially, the instinct of eating yields tremendous clarity, liberation and the security that you're eating the best foods for you – and only in the quantities you need – as well as generating profound, long-term health benefits. And it all happens through following your pleasure! We eat when we are hungry, stop when we've had enough, and know what we like and don't like, even if that changes by the minute. Our bodies provide endless entertainment and allow us to explore and play. We don't track grams, points, or exchanges, or worry about gluten or GMOs. We are blissfully unaware of the number on the scale or the little tag on our clothes. We are clear about our needs, intuitive and satisfied.

Somewhere along the way, the natural cues our bodies give us become harder to read. The world teaches us to eat when we aren't hungry. We learn this from TV commercials, social media, and our parents, who may say things like, "You can have this waffle if you finish your entire plate." As an adult, you continue this pattern. You've probably agreed to have lunch with someone, just to be social, when you weren't really hungry. You've probably been offered a second helping at a dinner party even after you told the host, "I'm totally stuffed!" On the other hand, diets encourage people to ignore their hunger level. They tell people to just tune out their hunger, which we all know is a recipe for disaster!

Chemical Senses – Taste and Smell

"Both taste and smell are what we call chemical senses. They operate by detecting minute amounts (molecules) of chemical substances. The sense of taste, also known as gustation, operates by detecting molecules in the air. Both taste and smell function in ways designed to help us survive." Alexander W. Logue (2015)

So, what happens if you eat a non-original food that no longer accurately communicates with your instincts? Let's take a look: A pineapple's smell and taste clearly reveal the essence of what that pineapple is, what its "nutrient makeup" is and what its subjective value to you is. However, pineapple tart is a different story. The smell, especially right out of the oven, no longer accurately represents the essence of the food. And because of the cooking process and the combining of many foods, the taste change is now either completely absent, muted or blurred. But your body is genetically programmed to "believe" that if something smells good you might need it and if it tastes good you do need it. So, it is totally natural to want to eat pineapple tart! Your body is following its innate intelligence. But the food is no longer living up to its end of the relationship by telling you the truth. It's saying to your instincts (via its always-attractive smell and taste) that it is an always-needed food. Well, this isn't always the case. And unfortunately, the symptoms of this tiny misunderstanding around food and instincts are displayed as immeasurable suffering worldwide.

As we all aware of, nowadays most of our dietary arts and sciences involve non-original food, eaten in a non-instinctive way. Additionally, they're tragically unrelated to our bio-instinctual system, which is prior to all the overlaid culinary systems. Because of this, we've developed boundless techniques for deciding what to eat, when to stop, and, indeed, what is considered food. These include endless diets, cultural dictates, weight loss and weight gain programs, using willpower to control eating, gluttony, eating disorders, guilt, shame – the list goes on and on. These are all sadly ineffective approaches compared to our inborn instinctive system, which can be trusted to handle all our food-selecting, eating and digesting with impeccable grace and effectiveness.

So, what's the cost for this relief? Basically, there is one primary discipline: Only eat foods whose smells and tastes accurately represent their essence and that also communicate an accurate taste change. Or as I like to say it, "I only eat foods that tell the truth." Practically speaking, this means selecting only from whole, raw and organic foods. This might sound like a frustrating limit. We will talk more about what is real food in Part IV: Nutrition.

There are also some secondary disciplines: Eat only one food at a time so that the taste change (or stop) on that particular food can be most easily "heard." And provide yourself with a wide range of original/real foods to choose from.

Imagine it's 50,000 years ago; our ancestors had to eat when food was available, because you never knew when food would be available again. It could be days or even weeks. Our primal instinct says, "Eat it now, I will store it as fat, so when we can't find food for a while, I will just burn the fat from this meal later." So, when our bodies have anything extra (i.e., the extra calories you get from consuming that donut), our bodies say, "Thank you very much, I am going to store this as fat to burn later when we are starving." But of course, nowadays, we never get to the point of starving, do we? We have food available at all times. So, most of us never in our lives get to the actual point of needing to burn that stored donut. Thus 53% of the world population is overweight and/or obese. Some of you might be thinking, "I will just starve myself for a few days to burn off the fat!" If only it were that easy! The lower your daily calorie intake, the less you burn! Again, that survival instinct kicks in. Once calories drop below the threshold of the energy needed to fuel basic bodily functions, the primal instinct kicks the body into survival mode. It starts shutting down all unnecessary systems and processes that normally burn energy to work. You guessed it right! Our bodies conserve energy - conservation of energy implies that the chemical energy stored in food is converted into work, thermal energy, and/or stored as chemical energy in fatty tissue. Hence, undoubtedly, our bodies go into slow metabolic burn and only fuel the basics. Stable blood sugar allows the body to stay in balance and consistently break down fat (homeostasis). That is how our survival instinct works against us.

Most of us have been trying to navigate the dietary maze in some form or other for quite some time. What I've found is that the body already knows the way. I invite you to explore your own body and instincts, and see if this message is validated in you. It might herald the beginning of a whole new sensibility around food, diet, health, and life altogether.

MAKING PEACE WITH FOOD

Food is the reason that some of us get out of bed, so happily in the morning.
It's the thing that nourishes us, it fuels us.
It keeps us going.
It's what warrants a midday break.
It brings us together.
It creates warmth, a welcoming feeling of community and a sense of belonging.
It can bring back memories and transport us to faraway places.
It brings happiness, comfort, and sometimes struggle.

Sometimes it can be a real struggle whether to eat this food or that. That food is bad, but this food is good; maybe just one bite of that food. I mean, it's not a big deal. It's just one bite.

What Do You Want From Food?

For most people, they have a list of everything that they want from food. Commonly when we ask people what they want from food, their answer is something like great health, longevity, vitality, energy, satisfaction, taste, pleasure, love, a lean body, less fat and more muscle, beauty, skin health, happiness, and more. These are the most common outcomes that we want from a relationship with food. Don't you agree that we really put the pressure on for food to deliver so many different kinds of benefits to us?

As in so many different kinds of relationships, one of the best ways to get what you want is to give it.

If you want satisfaction and energy from food, then bring that to the plate. If you want happiness and health, then put that into your food. Whatever bounty you expect from your meal, ask yourself, "How am I offering the very thing that I want in the relationship?" and the magic can begin to happen.

Then it's time to embrace your relationship with food in a whole new way in order to have food, health and personal evolution and excellence. Think of it as maturing into your relationship with food. Change and navigate the unknown for a better relationship with food.

How you show up for your relationship with food equally applies to your relationship with just about anything or anyone. Connect with the relationship, listen to the relationship, trust the relationship, work on the relationship, get help when you need it and don't rely on it too heavily for too many things – be reasonable. Also know that with any close relationship, there are always challenges, and places where we are asked to grow and mature.

Build Your Relationship with Food

Make peace with food. This involves getting rid of this feeling of guilt and shame and fear around eating, especially when eating foods that some people might call bad foods. Don't look at foods in such a binary way. When we tell ourselves that we can't have a certain food, it makes us mentally more preoccupied with that particular food and a little bit more obsessed with it. It gives it power, power that it really doesn't deserve. But if we instead give ourselves permission to eat any food, to be at peace with it, those foods start to lose their allure. So, the idea here is to give yourself permission to eat anything. So long as you're staying tuned in and listening to your body's cues.

I was so sceptical about this point when I first learned about it because I felt like it was just promoting a junk food diet. With that kind of permission without any boundaries or restrictions, I felt like it meant that you would lose all control. But the exact opposite is true. I remember the first time I decided to give the concept a try. I bought instant noodles and crackers to bring home. These were foods that I had previously not let myself bring home at all, and to be honest, the first few times I did overeat them, but even still, I kind of mustered up the courage to trust the process, and I kept bringing them into the house and then at some point, I don't know maybe a few weeks, maybe a few months later, I was sitting on the couch and

I was in the mood for a snack and then I remembered that we had two packs of instant noodles and crackers in the pantry. But then I realized I also wasn't in the mood for those things, and I wanted some fresh berries instead. The crackers that were once so exciting were things that I got exposed to over and over again and I kind of just habituated to them. So, when we make the doughnut as emotionally equivalent as the apple, for example, the doughnut loosens its grip over us. It makes the food emotionally neutral by allowing the foods to be there by permitting ourselves to have them. Maybe we will overeat them at first, but eventually, that novelty wears off and it gives us the permission to actually taste the food for what it is and to judge if we're even in the mood to have it at all.

Essentially, if you fuel your body with nutritious foods, your body will thank you in return because the food is there to nourish the cells but also to nourish the soul, and like a toddler, you no longer need to think about what you should be eating or feeling guilty about what you've just eaten. You can just enjoy the pleasure that you get from food, and when you're satisfied, just move on. It is all connected. Let's put it this way: you wouldn't want to invite a friend into your home you didn't get along with. In the same way, the food you are consuming needs to be nourishing and enhancing for your body.

You might not be aware of this but both the food you ingest and the way you feel about it can impact you and your life. We all know that if you eat something that doesn't agree with you, it can ruin your day. For example, have you ever indulged in a heavy piece of chocolate cake and felt ten times worse after? Consuming sugary foods can leave you feeling fatigued and stop you from operating productively. On the flipside, if you spend time lovingly preparing food for yourself and others, this tends to show up well in the body. For example, if you're feeling tired and opt for a green juice as opposed to a bubble tea, it can enhance the way you feel in that very moment.

PRACTICING FOOD MINDFULNESS

The word "mindfulness" is simply awareness of the present moment.

When you pause to observe what's happening right now—as if in slow motion—you not only have an opportunity to better understand why you do what you do, but you can also choose your actions rather than continue to react (re-act) out of habit. Instead of trying to stay in control and then subsequently losing control, mindfulness will help you learn to be in charge and give you response-ability. Mindfulness helps you recognize, then if needed, change the choices you make. As you discover a balance in the middle between the extremes, you'll gain the freedom to eat what you love, the awareness to eat what your body needs, the mindfulness to love what you eat, and the desire to meet your other needs in more satisfying ways than eating.

Mindful eating is one of the best practices when it comes to developing a better relationship with food. The first time the concept of mindful eating was introduced to the public was in 1990, in John Kabat-Zinn's best-selling book Full Catastrophe Living. He describes mindful eating in a few pages, including an activity on how to eat a raisin using a mindful approach.

Instead of following strict rules created by experts, practice food mindfulness to become the expert in you. You'll relearn how to use the fundamental information delivered by your hunger and fullness cues to determine when, what, and how much you need to eat.

THINK AND BE THIN

The Most Powerful Tool – Hunger Fullness Scale

Hunger fullness scale is the most sophisticated tool for not only telling you how much you need to eat but when. This is the tool designed to help you tune in with your own body. Zero and one on the scale is intense uncomfortable hunger, like when you feel empty and totally famished. Nine and ten on the scale are painfully stuffed, when you feel uncomfortably full to the point of being sick. But according to the scale, you want to begin eating when you feel a gentle or polite hunger, and that correlates with the three or four on the scale. When we eat when we feel a gentle hunger, we tend to be more rational with our food choices, maybe even making more wholesome food choices because we're not so famished. We also tend to eat more slowly.

We really take our time to enjoy the food, and as a result, we are more mindful, able to tune in and recognize when we're starting to feel comfortably full, which tends to be at around the six to seven range on the scale, which is where we would also ideally want to put a pause on eating.

Think about what happens to you when you let yourself get too hungry when you are at zero or one on the scale? When your hunger gives you a little nudge and you just hope it will go away. The more you ignore, the louder the hunger signs become, and the more agitated you feel. The longer you wait and fight it, the more you are likely to eat out of anger, frustration, or urgency. What types of food do you crave then? Naturally, you crave the fattiest, oiliest, cheesiest, deep fried things with fries and bubble tea. Sound familiar? What happens to your eating behaviour when you let yourself get too hungry? We're more likely to scarf down the plate, eating really quickly, and that can often swing us to a nine or ten on the fullness side of the scale. In fact, one of the biggest predictors of overeating is letting yourself get too hungry in the first place, which causes you to yo-yo between zero and ten; this is often what we see in people who binge and restrict these higher and lower values. This way of eating brings us feelings of discomfort. It doesn't feel very nice to be so hungry and then to be so full. The most important thing is that we start to understand fullness and what it can feel like to be comfortably full. If you come from a history of dieting, you might have learned to suppress those feelings of hunger and fullness. You might not even feel them anymore. That's completely normal and natural. It is possible to relearn it, but it does take time.

Hunger & Fullness Scale		
1	**Empty:** Weak & light-headed Stomach acid is churning.	The Hunger & Satiety Scale can be used as a way to monitor your eating habits. It also helps you to be more in touch with your body's natural hunger/satiety cues.
2	**Starving:** Very uncomfortable Feeling irritable & unable to concentrate	
3	**Fairly Hungry:** Uncomfortable stomach is rumbling	
4	**Slightly Hungry:** Barely uncomfortable Beginning to feel signs of hunger	By listening to your body's hunger/ satiety cues, you are better able to achieve a healthy weight.
5	**Neutral:** Comfortable More/less satisfied, but could eat a little more	
6	**Pleasantly Satisfied:** Perfectly comfortable Feel pleasantly satisfied	Begin eating when you're at 3 or 4. Stop at 5 if you're trying to lose weight. Stop at 6 if you're wanting to maintain your weight.
7	**Full:** Feel a little bit uncomfortable	
8	**Stuffed:** Uncomfortably full (Too full) Feel stuffed and even too full	Getting in touch with your body's natural hunger/ satiety cues. Simply remember to tune-in, listen to your body and honor your hunger and fullness.
9	**Bloated:** Very uncomfortably full. Need to loosed your clothes	
10	**Nauseous:** Not hungry at all	

	So full that you feel nauseous	

What, When, and How Much Do You Need to Eat?

"What should I eat?"
"When is the right time to eat?"
"How much should I eat?"

These are the most popular questions if you have experienced dieting before. Indeed, these questions are interrelated. Your choices, timing and amount of food are influenced by these three main factors. (I will just briefly summarize on the factors, because this topic by itself could be another book.)

Personal factors are defined as factors that are different from person to person. We can also call them individual factors. Some examples include taste preferences, genes, age, degree of nutrition information knowledge, and health status.

Environmental factors can also have an influence on our food choices. These are
aspects of a setting, atmosphere, or location that influence an individual's choices. Layout, marketing, climate, weather, price, and availability are examples of environmental factors.

Indirect factors outside of one's control may also affect food choices. For example, government policies might influence the cost to produce food, which may then be passed onto the consumer. The resulting changes in prices could in turn influence food purchases.

An individual could even be influenced by multiple factors at once, for example:
someone who hasn't eaten all day (hunger level), has little money to spend (personal income), and is running late to their second job (time) might choose a two-for-one special at a fast-food restaurant instead of cooking a healthy meal.

Let's go over an example. Grey and his daughter Emma are at a family barbecue.

Grey chose to eat spicy chicken wings and carrot salad. He avoids the green salad,

because it contains cilantro. Grey selects a plate of food for Emma. Emma eats a hot dog (but not the bun) and some fruit salad. She picks out all the honeydew and only eats the watermelon, grapes, and strawberries. Now let's discuss some examples of factors that may have influenced Grey and Emma's food choices. What do you think might have influenced their choices?

Let's look at personal factors impacting Emma's food choices: Let's begin with her taste preferences: Emma hates spicy food, loves watermelon and strawberries. The fact that she is at the age where children are typically resistant to trying new foods may also be a factor that influences her food choices. Some personal knowledge may also have an influence on her food choice. For example, Emma has heard that some foods help you run fast, which might make her want to eat these foods. An example of a genetic factor that may impact her food choice is the fact that Emma has a gene that makes cilantro taste bad. Now let's look at personal factors impacting Grey's food choices: Let's begin with his taste preferences: Grey loves spicy food, hates cilantro. The fact that he didn't eat breakfast and is very hungry by lunchtime most likely also impacted his food choices. Some personal knowledge may also have an influence on his food choice. For example, Grey knows that carrots are a good source of vitamin A. An example of a genetic factor that may impact his food choice is the fact that Grey, like Emma, has a gene that makes cilantro taste bad.

Now let's take a look at environmental factors impacting Emma and Grey's food

choices: There may be some agriculture factors that influenced Emma and Grey's choices. For example, watermelon and strawberries are in season. The placement of food can also be an environmental factor. For example, all the food is laid out on a single table. There is one long line to get food. Time is another factor. For example: Grey hurries when selecting food since others are waiting and Emma is hungry. The setting of the BBQ may also influence choice. For example, the barbecue is at a park and Emma rushes to eat her lunch, so she can play on the playground equipment. Park rules may also be a factor. For example, glass containers are prohibited, so Grey brings canned beverages. Finally, weather may be a factor: The fact that it is 35 degrees Celsius and humid are environmental factors that most likely will affect Grey and Emma's food choices.

It is important to note that many of these influences are not set in stone. Even personal taste preferences can change due to gene rules and the effects of experience on food preferences.

"What should I eat?"

You eat whatever you want. Instead of listening to others' opinions of what to eat, tune into your own body and feed your body what it was craving even if it is your favourite lasagne. When you listen to your body, your mind won't fill with judgement and guilt, and you will then find that your body actually craves nourishing food like vegetables and fruits. You naturally seek balance, assortment, and moderation in your eating.

Eat what you love. Let's be honest, food is wonderful! It is a simple, accessible, convenient way to add more pleasure to your life. Enjoying food is only a problem if it's your main source of pleasure.

All foods fit. When you're hungry, instead of turning to a long list of restricted and allowed foods, you could implement these 3 essentials B.A.M. principles – balance, assortment, moderation.

Principle One: Balance
Balance refers to the importance of providing your body with all its necessary nutrients. You have the flexibility of adjusting your intake from one meal to the next to achieve overall balance in your eating.

Principle Two: Assortment
Assortment refers to eating a variety of different foods. Eating the same foods all the time leads to monotony. Not only is it boring, it probably won't meet all your nutritional requirements. Assortment in

eating promotes overall health and enjoyment so it's important to eat from all the different food groups and to eat a variety of foods within each group.

Principle Three: Moderation

Moderation refers to how much and how often you eat certain things, but don't confuse it with weighing, measuring and calorie counting food. These extreme methods aren't necessary. The best way to determine if you've had enough to eat is to listen to your cues of hunger. Remember the hunger fullness scale? When your goal is to feel comfortable after eating, you're more likely to eat in moderation. When you are tuning in to your body, you are also more likely to choose unhealthy foods in moderation.

Always listen to your body:
- What do I want?
- What do I need?
- What do I have?

"When should I eat?"

When your body needs fuel, it triggers the physical sensations of hunger. You decide when to eat based on how hungry you are, but you also consider other factors like convenience, social norms, and the availability of appetizing food.

Knowing your level of hunger will help you identify how to accurately take care of the situation. To have a healthy relationship with food means that one is able to eat for the physiological reasons rather than emotional reasons and to stop eating at a point when the body and mind are truly satisfied. All hunger isn't created equal. There are different types and levels. Obviously, being a little hungry is very different from feeling starved. If you are a little hungry, a snack rather than a full meal is the perfect antidote.

This is what I call "real hunger." Physical hunger stems from a need for energy from food. Just like when our bladder stretches, it signals a need to pee, or when our mouth feels dry, it signals a need to hydrate, when we feel the physical signs of hunger, it means we need food.

We normally think of hunger as an empty or gnawing sensation in the stomach, but you can also experience signs of hunger outside the stomach. Sometimes physical hunger can present as fatigue, anxiety, headaches, shakiness, or just thinking more about food. The only way to take care of physical hunger is to eat!

At times, you may become disconnected from the physical sensations of hunger so you don't recognize, pay attention to, or respond to the signals. Perhaps you feel like you're hungry all the time. Wanting to eat isn't the same thing as needing to eat.

Could you be misinterpreting other physical symptoms and sensations like thirst, fatigue, or nervousness for hunger?

Do you confuse emotional or environmental triggers, cravings, and appetite with hunger? Maybe you never feel hungry.

Could you be missing the signals of hunger because you don't really remember how hunger feels or you're too busy or distracted to notice?

Have you learned to ignore hunger because of dieting or wanting to maintain a certain weight?

Or maybe you really aren't hungry because you're eating for so many other reasons.

What are all the signs your body gives you to let you know when you need to eat? Do you recognize any of these common hunger symptoms?

- Growling or grumbling in the stomach
- Empty or hollow feeling
- Slight queasy feeling
- Weakness or loss of energy
- Trouble concentrating
- Difficulty making decisions
- Light headedness
- Slight headache

- Shakiness
- Feeling that you must eat as soon as possible

Did you know your brain has a built-in My Fitness Pal called the hypothalamus, which can sense energy intake and regulates appetite in response to your energy needs? Just like the urge to pee means you need to urinate, a dry mouth tells you to drink water, and heavy eyes tell you to sleep (or drink coffee), hunger means you need food. It really is as simple as that.

So, when it comes to a healthy weight, when it comes to energy levels, when it comes to your ability to have a good mood and stamina to get through the day, learning how to eat when you first get hungry and stopping at fulness is the foundation. Although what you eat is important, it turns out when you eat is just as important, and for some of us, it's even more important.

"How much should I eat?"

You might have heard of the expression, what gets measured gets managed. I personally love the expression. I think it holds very true, and I think it's expressions like this one that encourage some people to measure their weight or to track their intake by counting calories or macros. One thing that's important to know is that these tools help us measure external variables. And so that means that often it's not helping us stay in tune with what's happening inside of our bodies. If anything, they might even make us neglect those inner signals. But I do get the allure of using tools because they give us a sense and a feeling of control.
They let us know whether or not we're making improvements.

So instead of tracking our weight or calories, there's another tool that we can use to manage our intake, and it's a tool I personally think is a lot more powerful - the hunger and fullness scale

You decide how much food to eat by how hungry you are, how filling the food is, how soon you'll be eating again, and other factors. When your hunger is satisfied, you usually stop eating—even if there's food left. You recognize that being too full is uncomfortable and unnecessary.

For example, when you're disconnected from hunger and fullness and you overeat for emotional reasons, it may actually feel good, at least temporarily. However, when you're aware and more connected, you'll feel physically uncomfortable and recognize that eating did not meet your emotional needs very well. To change old patterns, you'll need to rediscover how great it feels when you don't overeat and learn what to do on those occasions when you do. It's important to tune into your thoughts, feelings, and behaviors without judgement. You're not going through this process to punish yourself but to see what you can learn from the experience.

Compare teaching yourself to eat just the right amount of food to teaching a child to ride a bike. Do children learn easily when you get angry or criticize them for making mistakes? Will children feel like giving up if they are expected to do it perfectly right away? Will they want to try again if they're ashamed about falling off? Or do they learn best when you observe what they do, encourage each positive step they take, and offer gentle suggestions on how they can improve? Do they want to keep trying because you focus on how much they are progressing, not on what they do wrong? Will they feel encouraged when they notice it gets a little easier each time? Learning to stop eating when you're satisfied is exactly the same. You're most likely to learn when you're gentle, patient, encouraging, and optimistic with yourself throughout the process. And, as with riding a bike, this process eventually becomes natural. Occasionally, something will throw you off balance, but because you've practiced and learned to make necessary adjustments and corrections, you'll keep cruising right along.

Enough is enough. As we've worked our way to practice food mindfulness, you've learned the powerful tool to help you eat the amount of food your body needs. You learned that mindfulness requires intention and attention. Your intention is to meet your body's needs and to feel better when you're finished than you did when you started—in other words, satisfied. You pay attention to enjoy eating even more. You fell somewhere between very full to sick and very uncomfortable from overeating.

THINK AND BE THIN

	Factors of Influence	Mindfulness Approach
What should I eat?		
When is the right time to eat?	Personal factors Environmental factors Indirect factors	B.A.M principles Hunger fullness scale
How much should I eat?		

CHAPTER 11

THE COMPASSIONATE INSTINCT

It is hard to accept your body wisdom – the instinctive ability when it comes to food if you are unrealistic and overly critical of your body shape. As long as you are at war within your body, it will be difficult to be at peace with yourself and food. Studies have shown that the more you focus on your body, the worse you feel about yourself. Yet the body torture game goes on. "Mirror, mirror on the wall, who's the slimmest of them all?"

BEFRIEND YOURSELF

This kind of compulsive concern with "I, me, and mine" isn't the same as loving
ourselves . . . Loving ourselves points us to capacities of resilience, compassion, and understanding within that are simply part of being alive. —Sharon Salzberg, The Force of Kindness

Modern society is becoming more and more competitive. How many of us truly feel good about ourselves? Anything less seems like a failure. Most of us are incredibly harsh on ourselves when we finally admit some shortcoming. "I'm not good enough. I'm worthless." It's not surprising that we hide the truth from ourselves when honesty is met with such harsh condemnation.

In areas where it is hard to fool ourselves, when comparing our weight to those of social influencers, we cause ourselves incredible amounts of emotional pain.

Even if we do manage to get our act together, the goalposts for what counts as "good enough" seem always to remain frustratingly out of reach. We must be smart and fit and fashionable and interesting and successful and sexy. And no matter how well we do, someone else always seems to be doing it better than us. The result of this line of thinking is sobering, causing millions of people to take pharmaceuticals every day just to cope with daily life. Insecurity, anxiety, and depression are incredibly common in our society, and much of this is due to self-judgment, to beating ourselves up when we feel we aren't winning in the game of life.

Self-compassion is very important when it comes to long-term weight-loss success. Self-compassion requires that we stop to recognize our own suffering. We can't be moved by our own pain if we don't even acknowledge that it exists in the first place. Of course, sometimes the fact that we're in pain is blindingly obvious, and we can think of nothing else. More often than you might think, however, we don't recognize when we are suffering. If we're in a difficult or stressful situation, we rarely take the time to step back and recognize how hard it is for us in the moment. And when our pain comes from self-judgment, if you're angry at yourself for overeating, or for eating unhealthy food at a wedding party, it's even harder to see these as moments of suffering.

Like the time I asked a friend, Lena, whom I hadn't seen in a while, eyeing the bump of her belly, "Are we expecting? When is your due date?"

"Er, no," she answered, "I've just put on some weight."

"Oh . . ." I said as my face turned beet red. We typically don't recognize such moments as a type of pain that is worthy of a compassionate response. After all, I messed up. Doesn't that mean I should be punished? Well, do you punish your friends or your family when they mess up? Okay, maybe sometimes a little, but do you feel good about it?

Everybody makes mistakes at one time or another; it's a fact of life. And if you think about it, why should you expect anything different? Where is that written contract you signed before birth promising that you'd be a perfect human, that you'd never fail, and that your life would go absolutely the way you want it to?

Most of our self-critical thoughts take the form of an inner dialogue, a constant self-talk and evaluation of what we are experiencing. Because there is no social censure when our inner dialogue is harsh, we often talk to ourselves in an especially brutal way. "You're so fat and disgusting!" "That was a totally stupid thing to do." "You're such a loser. No wonder nobody wants you." Yet such self-abuse is incredibly common. Floccinaucinihilipilification, defined as the habit of estimating something as worthless, is one of the longest words in the English language. The mystery of why we do it is as baffling as how to pronounce it.

Rather than condemning yourself for your mistakes and failures, you can use the experience of suffering to soften your heart. You can let go of those unrealistic expectations of perfection that make you so dissatisfied, and open the door to real and lasting satisfaction by giving yourself the compassion you need in the moment.

Practicing self-compassion when it comes to food means that we do the best we can to choose foods that are worthy of us. We don't judge ourselves too harshly when things go a little off course. Instead, we treat ourselves like we would treat a good friend who came to us and said, "I've been eating terribly. I've had no time to exercise, and I can't seem to break this cycle." If you're a good friend, you would likely reassure that friend, encourage them and maybe even support them in making some sustainable changes. Why are we often less forgiving with ourselves? The main message of this side of the self-compassion triangle is, instead of judging yourself, be kind and encouraging to yourself. Self-compassion also means recognizing that everybody makes less than optimal decisions once in a while, and that when you do, you're not alone. Most people struggle to navigate our confusing food landscape. In fact, an entire field of research is dedicated to exploring how people navigate the modern food environment. Recognizing and internalizing a sense of shared struggle or common humanity is the second of the three sides of the self-compassion triangle. Basically, you're not alone. The struggles you face are shared by many others. The final side of the self-compassion triangle has to do with mindful noting. It means that when we get off track with anything and we find ourselves disappointed with our decisions, we don't allow that disappointment to define us. Instead of over identifying with the feeling of disappointment, you just acknowledge it for what it is, a feeling, and move on. You are not your doubts, you are not your disappointments or your frustration. So don't let them define you.

Self-compassion is a gift available to anyone willing to open up to themselves. When we develop the habit of self-kindness, suffering becomes an opportunity to experience love and tenderness from within. No matter how difficult things get, we can always wrap our torn and tattered selves in our own soft embrace. We can soothe and comfort our own pain, just as a child is soothed and comforted by her mother's arms. We don't have to wait until we are perfect, until life goes exactly as we want it to. We don't need others to respond with care and compassion in order to feel worthy of love. We don't need to look outside ourselves for the acceptance and security we crave. This is not to say that we don't need other people. Of course, we do. But who is in the best position to know how you really feel underneath that cheerful façe? Who is most likely to know the full extent of the pain and fear you face, to know what you need most? Who is the only person in your life who is available 24/7 to provide you with care and kindness? You.

HONOUR YOUR BODY

What does body image really mean? Does the phrase conjure feelings of security, love and value, or does it inflict feelings of shame and a desire to alter oneself?

Your body image is what you think and how you feel when you look in the mirror or when you picture yourself in your mind. This includes how you feel about your appearance and what you think about your body itself, such as your height and weight, and how you feel within your own skin. Body image also includes how you behave as a result of your thoughts and feelings. You may have a positive or negative body image. Body image is not always related to your weight or size.

It is important to remember that everybody is different. We all have different genetic and cultural traits. Even if everyone started eating the same things and did the same amount of exercise for a whole year, we would not all look the same at the end of the year. This is because each person's genetic inheritance influences their bone structure, body size, shape, and weight differently.

Women with a positive body image are more likely to have good physical and mental health. Girls and women with negative thoughts and feelings about their bodies are more likely to develop certain mental health conditions, such as eating disorders and depression. Researchers think that dissatisfaction with their bodies may be part of the reason more women than men have depression.

A negative body image may also lead to low self-esteem, which can affect many areas of your life. You may not want to be around other people or you may obsess constantly about what you eat or how much you exercise. But you can take steps to develop a healthier body image.

Women who are obese are more likely to have a negative body image, but not all women who are obese or overweight are dissatisfied with their bodies. Women with a healthy weight can also have a negative body image, although obesity can make a woman's negative body image more severe.

Weight is not the only part of a person's body that determines body image. Self-esteem, past history, daily habits such as grooming, and the particular shape of your body all contribute to body image.

Weight is an important part of body image, but it is not the only part.

One list cannot automatically tell you how to turn negative body thoughts into positive body image, but it can introduce you to healthier ways of looking at yourself and your body. The more you practice these new thought patterns, the better you will feel about who you are and the body you naturally have.

Tip #1: Appreciate all that your body can do.
Every day, your body carries you closer to your dreams. Celebrate all the amazing things your body does for you—running, dancing, breathing, laughing, dreaming, etc.

Tip #2: Remind yourself that "true beauty" is not skin-deep.
When you feel good about yourself and who you are, you carry yourself with a sense of confidence, self-acceptance, and openness that makes you beautiful. Beauty is a state of mind, not a state of your body.

Tip #3: Look at yourself as a whole person.
When you see yourself in a mirror or in your mind, choose not to focus on specific body parts. See yourself as you want others to see you — as a whole person. Keep a top-ten list of things you like about yourself, things that aren't related to how much you weigh or what you look like. Read your list often. Add to it as you become aware of more things to like about yourself.

Tip #4: Become a critical viewer of social media messages.
Pay attention to images, slogans, or attitudes that make you feel bad about yourself or your body. Protest these messages: write a letter to the advertiser or talk back to the image or message. Shut down those voices in your head that tell you your body is not "right" or that you are a "bad" person. You can overpower those negative thoughts with positive ones. The next time you start to tear yourself down, build yourself back up with a few quick affirmations that work for you.

Tip #5: Do something nice for yourself.
Do something that lets your body know you appreciate it. Take a bubble bath, make time for a nap, or find a peaceful place outside to

relax. Use the time and energy that you might have spent worrying about food, calories, and your weight to do something to help others. Sometimes reaching out to other people can help you feel better about yourself and make a positive change in our world.

CHAPTER 12

kNOw DIETING MENTALITY

"Your mind is the most powerful partner you have for creating healthy metabolism function. In fact, it's the energetic engine that drives metabolism function. Can you appreciate your body's oneness and inseparability? The healthful choices we make in terms of beliefs support the highest level of metabolism function. Remember this simple truth: If you always associate with the good, you will become the good. If you associate with the negative, you become the negative. This is the real power of attraction that energetic frequencies exert on each other. You can improve your metabolism function every day by choosing positive, kind, healthful beliefs. When beliefs change, the same eyes can look at the same reality and see different things. Then, different outcomes are possible." –Digesting the Universe: A Revolutionary Framework for Healthy Metabolism Function, by Nan Lu, OMD with Ellen Schaplowsky

A study by a digestive physiologist tells us that indeed, digestion begins in the mind. There is a scientific term called the cephalic phase digestive response. This is a fancy way of saying that there's a component of digestion that begins in the mind. Cephalic means of the head. The cephalic phase digestive response is essentially the components of taste, pleasure, aroma, satisfaction, and the visuals of a meal.

Think of a time when you looked at a favorite food and your mouth started to water. That's the cephalic phase digestive response in action – you're producing more saliva and salivary amylase just from a visual cue.

The bottom line is this: the brain and its thinking have far-reaching effects in nutritional metabolism. Science tells us that approximately 40 to 60% of our metabolic power at any meal, meaning our digestive and assimilative ability, comes from the head phase of digestion – meaning taste, pleasure, aroma, satisfaction, and visual cues.

Now, please do the math.

If we're not receiving and experiencing the head phase of digestion, then we're metabolizing our meal at 40 to 60% less efficiency.

How often do you come across diet books, magazine articles, and programs that offer you the false hope of losing weight quickly, easily, and permanently? All these give you fake hopes and lead you to feel as if you are a failure when a new diet stops working and you gain back all the weight. Dieting rarely works; 95% of all dieters regain their lost weight and more within 1 to 5 years.

Once a client told me she went through a 30-day challenge conducted by a certified nutritionist, it was a restrictive or conventional type of diet challenge. In the program, she was told to drink raw vegetable blended juice daily and to only eat vegetables and a little portion of carbohydrates throughout the 30 days. This kind of challenge will definitely help you to shed pounds after the 30 days, but is this a healthy approach? Is this sustainable? Can you survive with this kind of diet throughout your life? You got it, this client come to me and asked for a private coaching session a few months after the 30-day challenge because she literally put on more weight. I shifted her mindset with all the techniques and tools I'm sharing with you in this book right now, using the T.H.I.N. Transformation Blueprint.

Three days before the coaching session, she kept asking me what foods to eat and what foods not to eat. I shared with her my 30-day flexible meal plan (no restriction), and told her just to use it as a guideline, that she may not need to follow the meal plan but just eat normally. Additionally, I got her to follow through my online program. On day 7 after my coaching session, she texted me, "My body feels very good after breakfast, not too heavy, not sleepy, in fact, I feel my brain is clear and energetic!"

For most people, being told no dieting can be scary! A study by Diet Chef revealed that a woman will spend a shocking total of 17 years of her lifetime trying to lose weight on a diet. Dieting people are caught in between these conflicting fears, "If I continue dieting, I'll ruin my metabolism and gain weight. But if I stop dieting, I'll gain more weight."

Dieter's Dilemma

The dieter's dilemma is triggered with the realization of being overweight and deciding to set a goal to be slim, which leads to dieting. The dieter is committed to following the restrictive diet hoping to get instant results without knowing that the results won't last for long, and she'll eventually regain the weight due to cheeky rewards of losing control for overeating.

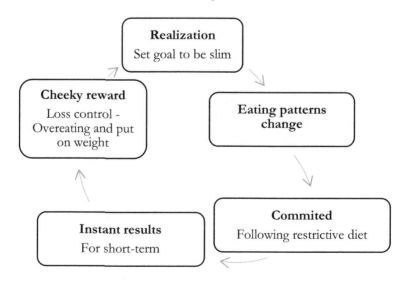

Although antidieting movement is growing in popularity, there is always a new diet or program popping up every now and then. You must simply make the decision to give up dieting, but how?

Tip #1: Acknowledge the Damage from Dieting

Based on a report by National Eating Disorders Association of U.S., "yo-yo" dieting, a repeating cycle of gaining, losing and regaining weight, has been shown to have negative health effects, including increased risk of heart disease and long-lasting negative impacts on metabolism. Dieting forces your body into starvation mode. It responds by slowing down many of its normal functions to conserve energy. This means your natural metabolism actually slows down. Dieters often miss out on important nutrients. For example, dieters often don't get enough calcium, leaving them at risk for osteoporosis, stress fractures and broken bones.

Dieters often experience physical consequences such as:
- loss of muscular strength and endurance
- decreased oxygen utilization
- thinning hair
- loss of coordination
- dehydration and electrolyte imbalances
- fainting, weakness, and slowed heart rates

Dieting also impacts your mind. When you restrict calories, you restrict your energy, which in turn can restrict your brainpower. Medical studies indicate that people on diets have slower reaction times and a lesser ability to concentrate than people not on a diet. All the stress and anxiety about food and weight that preoccupy dieters actually can consume a portion of a dieter's working memory capacity. Numerous studies link chronic dieting with feelings of depression, low-self-esteem and increased stress.

Dieting can lead to eating disorders. Many studies and many health professionals note that patients with eating disorders were dieting at the time of the development of their eating disorder. Dieting may not cause an eating disorder, but the constant concern about body weight and shape, fat grams and calories can start a vicious cycle of body dissatisfaction and obsession that can lead all too quickly to an eating disorder.

Tip #2: S.T.O.P. skill

The thought patterns of the dieter and non-dieter are different in the way they view eating, exercise and the progress of achieving healthy weight.

When it comes to eating or food choices, the dieter always feel guilty when he or she eats heavy foods. Dieters usually describe a day of eating as either good or bad. Dieters also view food as the enemy. While a non-dieter will access foods in a different aspect, they will know whether it is real hunger they feel and whether the food tastes good; they will enjoy eating without guilt.

The dieter will focus on the calories burned during exercise and eventually feel guilty if they miss a designated exercise day. The no-dieter focus primarily on how exercise makes them feel, especially the energizing and stress-relieving factors.

In view of the progress of losing weight, the dieter will constantly check on the pounds lost, the physical look and what other people think or judge of her weight. A non-dieter will not take weight on the scale as the primary goal or indicator of progress. They increase trust within themselves and with food, as they are able to recognize inner body cues.

Mindfulness is one of the successful therapies for self-help. Mindfulness was first applied in healthcare by Dr. John Kabat-Zinn in 1970s as an 8-week mindfulness-based stress reduction (MBSR) programme for managing chronic pain at the University of Massachusetts Medical Centre, U.S. Mindful-S.T.O.P. is an acronym for a four-step approach that can be used to "log in" and conveniently cultivate mindfulness at anytime and anywhere.

Step 1: S - STOP
Stop whatever that you are doing and the business of the mind

and gently allow your attention to return to and rest in the present moment.

This is how one can train the mind to unlock itself from a compulsive doing mode or mindless mode.

Step 2: T – TAKE DEEP & MINDFUL BREATHS

Take 3 slow deep breaths and allow your attention to rest on the movement of your breath.

Mindful breathing is useful for anchoring our attention on the present moment, instead of getting lost in dieting thoughts.

Step 3: O – OBSERVE THE PRESENT MOMENT

Observe the present moment as you are breathing in and out, such as the sounds around you (fan, people talking) or sights (flower, buildings) or sensations (hands and steering while driving).

This enables us to temporarily disengage from our busy thoughts, and shift our attention to a "free gear" mode, resting and relaxing in the present moment.

Step 4: P – PROCEED WITH A SMILE

Proceed with whatever you need to do with a smile.

Smiling has been known to relax the mind-body, to facilitate helpful thoughts and to improve interpersonal relationships. When the mind is calm and in smiley mode, problem solving is likely to be more effective.

Next time the dieting desire crosses your mind, use the Mindful S.T.O.P. skill for easy and immediate self-help.

Tip #3: Empty Your Cup

One of the stories you might have already heard about is this. Back in 1964, author Joe Hyams met with the legendary Bruce Lee for the very first time to see if Sensei Lee would teach him privately.
"Why do you want to study with me?" Bruce asked.
"Because I was impressed with your demonstration and because I've heard you are the best."
"You've studied other martial arts?" he asked.
"For a long time," Joe answered, "but I stopped some time ago and now I want to start over again."
"Do you realize you will have to unlearn all you have learned and start over again?" he asked.
"No," Joe said.

Bruce smiled and placed his hand lightly on Joe's shoulder. "Let me tell you a story my sifu told me," he said. "It is about the Japanese Zen master who received a university professor who came to inquire about Zen. It was obvious to the master from the start of the conversation that the professor was not so much interested in learning about Zen as he was in impressing the master with his own opinions and knowledge. The master listened patiently and finally suggested they have tea. The master poured his visitor's cup full and then kept on pouring. The professor watched the cup overflowing until he could no longer restrain himself. 'The cup is overfull, no more will go in.' 'Like the cup,' the master said, 'you are full of your own opinions and speculations. How can I show you Zen unless you first empty your cup?'"
Bruce studied Joe's face. "You understand the point?"
"Yes," I said. "You want me to empty my mind of past knowledge and old habits so that I will be open to new learning."
"Precisely," said Bruce. "And now we are ready to begin your first lesson."

Many a time we bring a lot of "baggage" with us when we want to learn something. We carry beliefs, expectations, perspectives, opinions and pre-conceived ideas when learning. How are we meant to learn when we already know so much? Three most dangerous words one could ever utter when learning is, "I know that." Once those words are said, very little information is able to penetrate into the mind, for the mind is already full and closed.

There are various reasons why we do that. Sometimes, we do not want to appear stupid. Maybe it is because we feel we are expected to know that. Maybe we are too shy to ask or to admit our ignorance. Maybe we are not interested in learning more. Maybe we really think we know it all.

Knowledge is truly boundless. Imagine if you are sitting in a room, say, the exact room you are in now. Where you are sitting is what you know you know. Around the room is what you know you do not know. For example, if there is a cupboard or storage in the room, you know there is something inside but you also know you do not know what is inside. Or if there is a person carrying a bag or having pockets, you know there is something in there but you do not know what it is. So, you know what you do not know. Now, outside the room, you have no idea what is happening out there, which means you do not know what you do not know. Someone once said, "Two things are infinite: the universe and human stupidity, and I am not yet completely sure about the universe." We simply do not know everything. To think that we do is just plain arrogant and silly.

If we truly want to learn, we need to empty our cup. No matter how full, it is a prerequisite to learning. The usefulness of a cup is its emptiness. To better improve our skills on weight management, we need to empty our cups to learn from each other. Education is a two-way thing. The best masters are also the best students. The more I learn about anything, the more I realise I know nothing.

PART 4: NUTRITION (EAT YOUR WAY THIN)

CHAPTER 13

FUEL YOUR BODY

MY PARENTS' POULTRY FARM & VEGETABLE FARM

My memories of seeing my parents coming in wet from the morning vegetables pick in the very early days of farming are still fresh and clear. Even now, after living in the city of Kuala Lumpur, I still think of myself as a farm girl or village girl, happiest when I'm around chilis and bugs and rivers. My parents farmed as a side income when I was a little kid. Mom and Dad worked all the time, and we lived simply. My dad used to own a poultry farm; he kept chickens and fish in a pond, and he had to let go due to dishonest business partner. In many ways it was a hard life. But however sore and tired they were, they loved farming, and for us kids, the farm was a rusty, dusty paradise embracing both work and goofing off.

It can be very satisfying to grow your own food and enjoy the fruits of your work directly. It's also a great way to experience and learn more about nature.

Nowadays, for those who live in the city, small gardens and even balconies can be enough space to grow food, such as tomatoes or strawberries. If you don't have access to a garden, you could plant salad leaves or herbs in a window box or in a plant pot. If you have enough space, on the other hand, why not go big on a vegetable plot and save on your shopping bill at the same time? You may also find that in your local area, there are opportunities to share an allotment, or even community gardens or food growing projects. That will allow you to share the labour and the fruits, as well as learn from others in a social environment. And there are also immediate opportunities to pick your own food, by going fruit picking or foraging for wild food. Look for local farms, including city farms or orchards that let you pick fruit to buy.

My parents still work on the farm with free-range chickens, various type of vegetables and local fruits like bananas, and passionfruit; it is their hobby. They also farm at the side of our corner lot house. Simply picking up some vegetables before dinner is what we do most of the time. We are so lucky to be able to enjoy fresh vegetables and local fruits every now and then. I'm so grateful that my omnivorous parents were the healthiest people I knew, lean and cheerful in their 60s as they tucked into fried eggs and pork chops.

FOOD WITHOUT LABEL

Real food is food without a label. It is whole, single-ingredient food. It is mostly unprocessed, free of chemical additives and rich in nutrients. Real food is food that hasn't been artificially created. It has grown in soil and/or had a mother.

Real food doesn't have ingredients; real food is ingredients. – Jamie Oliver

In essence, it's the type of food human beings ate exclusively for thousands of years. Think of real food like "normal" food, food that our great grandparents ate before mankind learned how to create artificial preservatives, colors, and make processed foods, with the sole purpose to generate a lot of money.

Don't eat anything your great-grandmother wouldn't recognize as food. – Michael Pollan

In the definition of real food, no food is bad food. Steak, beans, yogurt – all are examples of real food.

*Real beef is raised on grass (not soybeans) and aged properly.
*Real milk is grass-fed, raw, and unhomogenized, with the cream on top.
*Real eggs come from hens that eat grass, grubs, and bugs, not "vegetarian" hens.
*Real lard is never hydrogenated, as industrial lard is.
*Real olive oil is cold-pressed, leaving vitamin E and antioxidants intact.
*Real tofu is made from fermented soybeans, which are more digestible.
*Real bread is made with yeast and allowed to rise, a form of fermentation.
*Real grits are stone-ground from whole corn and soaked with soda before cooking.

People everywhere love real foods or sometimes they call them traditional foods. They're fond of a nice steak, the crispy skin of roast chicken, or mashed potatoes made with plenty of milk and butter. But they're afraid that eating these things might make them fat, or worse, give them a heart attack. So, they do as they're told by the experts: they drink skim milk and order egg white omelets. Their favorite foods become a guilty pleasure. I believe the experts are wrong; the real culprits in heart disease are not real foods but industrial ones, such as margarine, powdered eggs, refined corn oil, and sugar. Real food is good for you.

How healthy is healthy? You can never go wrong with real food. But it's not as easy as it seems. The supermarket is stacked with bags and boxes of edibles that aren't actually real food, but they are labeled as natural or healthy foods. Don't get confused by labels like "natural," "gluten-free," and "low-fat." The food industry bombards you with thousands of options, which leads to confusion and often poor choices. The health halo effect occurs when you see a label on the front of a package that says "good source of vitamin C" and believe that it is automatically better for you or lower in calories. These claims can actually mean very little, but we often believe that they are better for us. We want to do the right thing for ourselves and our families, but it gets harder all the time. Your best bet is to investigate the product for yourself by looking at the nutrition facts label that can be found on each item. Or, better yet, aim for minimally processed foods with as few ingredients as possible. How to know whether what you're eating is made up of actual food? Ask yourself three questions:

1. Does it have fewer than 3 ingredients?
2. Can you conjure up a vision of what each ingredient looks like in its natural state (i.e., tomato, chili)?
3. Will it start rotting if you let it sit on your shelf for two weeks?

HIGHEST, MEDIUM and LOWEST STRATEGIES

Nutrition is a very broad and very personal subject. After all, we make choices about our food and our family's food every day, several times a day. Basic nutritional knowledge will help when making food choices. You need to eat more of the highest quality types of proteins, carbohydrates and fats.

"Consume essential nutrients in the right amount plus the foods you love because you are you."

Protein Power

Pick your protein, such as tofu, wild salmon, or an omega-3 powerhouse food. Pick SMASH, an acronym for foods that are high in omega-3: sardines, mackerel, anchovies, salmon, and herring.

At least 10,000 different proteins helped to build your body and help to maintain it. With genetic codes as a blueprint, protein is built from essential and nonessential amino acids.

Complete proteins contain all the essential amino acids that we need to build new proteins. These are mostly of animal origin; the exception is soybean and quinoa. Incomplete proteins are missing an essential amino acid or do not contain an adequate amount; these include bread, nuts, rice, beans, and vegetables. You can combine proteins to complete incomplete proteins.

Highest Quality: **Least Processed and Least Refined**
Fish Chicken Beef Eggs Quinoa Soybean
Medium Quality: **Medium Processed and Medium Refined**
Canned Meat Cheese Yogurt Sandwich Meats Soy Meat – Packaged Cottage Cheese
Low Quality: **Most Processed and Most Refined**
Protein Powder Protein Bar

Are Carbs the Enemy?

The trouble with carbohydrates lies in our food selection and our changing food supply. The shift in the food landscape has been associated with the development of chronic illness, most notably type 2 diabetes. The function of carbohydrates is to ensure the optimum functioning of the body. Bodies have many defenses against having inadequate amounts of carbohydrates because they are the exclusive fuel of brains and muscles.

Choose your carbohydrates wisely. If they are associated with a whole grain, it is an advantageous form of carbohydrate. Make wiser carbohydrate choices by reducing the consumption of all sweet drinks. Add complex carbohydrates to your diet like vegetables, legumes, dried beans, and peas.

Highest Quality: **Least Processed and Least Refined**
Fresh Beans Brown Rice Fruit Vegetables Yams Millets
Medium Quality: **Medium Processed and Medium Refined**
Bread Canned Beans Crackers Pasta Pretzels Potatoes
Low Quality: **Most Processed and Most Refined**
Ice Cream Potato Chips Tortilla Chips White Rice

Fat Facts

Not all fats are bad. Omega-3 fatty acids were the solution for an athlete who had inflammation in his joints and was struggling with pain. We will explore how fats are neither good nor evil, look at some essential terminology, discuss the consequences of the types of dietary fats, and discuss the basic functions of fat in the diet.

First, some terminology and general facts about fat. Fats are the most energy dense of all the macronutrients, at 9 calories per gram. Chemically, fats are made up of 3 elements: carbon, hydrogen, and oxygen. Saturated fats have a long carbon fatty-acid chain full of hydrogen ions. Unsaturated fats have double bonds that exist between carbon molecules. Trans fats are unsaturated vegetable oils that manufacturers hydrogenate to make more solid so that they last longer. More than 90% of the fat in our body is triglycerides, which are 3 fatty acids stuck to a glycerol backbone. Cholesterol technically does not contain fatty acids, but it is classified as a lipid because it has some of the same chemical and physical characteristics as lipids.

What are the functions of fat? Fat is an energy source. It provides thermal insulation that protects the vital organs from trauma. Fat serves as a vitamin carrier and hunger depressor. Fat is necessary for the production of many regulatory hormones. Fat is necessary for the production of structural components, such as brain development and function.

What is the difference between good and bad fat? Total fat has declined in the American diet, but the average American is still consuming about 15% of total calories as saturated fat despite the recommended intake of 10% or less. In the typical American diet, saturated fat is 34% from plant sources and the rest is from animal sources. Health professionals recommend replacing some of the saturated fat and all trans fats with nonhydrogenated monounsaturated and polyunsaturated fats. Essential fatty acids are omega-3 fatty acids, which are found in the oils of cold-water fish and flaxseed oil, and omega-6 fatty acids, which are found in meat, corn oil, safflower oil, and sunflower oil.

There are no firm dietary needs or standards for fat. The American Heart Association encourages people to focus on replacing high-fat foods with vegetables, fruit, poultry, lean meat, unrefined whole grains, and fat-free or low-fat dairy products. They recommend the omega-3 fatty acids in fish. The American Heart Association and other organizations also recommend no more than 300 mg of cholesterol per day. The American Cancer Society is more aggressive and encourages a diet that contains only 20% of total calories from lipids to reduce the risk of certain types of cancer. A prudent recommendation is that 30% or less of your total calories should be from fat, and the majority should be unsaturated fat.

Let's look at fat deficiencies and excesses. Inadequate absorption of fat may be due to steatorrhea, which can result in severe vitamin states. Very low-fat diets can be associated with gallstones. Some of the disease states associated with fat excess will be discussed in later lectures.

Highest Quality: Least Processed and Least Refined
Avocado
Flaxseed Oil
Natural Nut Butter
Nuts
Olive Oil

Medium Quality: Medium Processed and Medium Refined
Canola Oil
Canned Olives
Processed Nut Butters

Low Quality: Most Processed and Most Refined
Butter
Margarine
Mayonnaise
Salad Dressing
Sour Cream

STAY HYDRATED

We were taught that we need eight 8-ounce glasses of water per day. For some of us, this is not enough, and for others, it overestimates our needs. Our bodies are about 65%–70% water, but less so if you have more body fat because body fat is anhydrous. The function of water goes beyond refreshment. It serves as a transport vehicle and lubricant, provides the moisture for tears, and regulates heat loss.

The majority of water is stored around the cells and in the bloodstream. The average adult eliminates about 2.5 liters of water a day. Our food consumption is a source of fluid—about 17 ounces per day. Drinking 2 liters of fluid per day keeps most people hydrated.

To test your hydration level, check your urine color. It should look like pale lemonade. Thirst is a poor measure of hydration because there is a lag between the time you get dehydrated and the time you actually experience thirst. Also, the older we get, the less sensitive the thirst mechanism is.

The American College of Sports Medicine gives guidelines on what to drink. If you exercise less than an hour at moderate intensity, water is fine while you are exercising. If you are exercising out in the heat for more than 30 minutes, you probably need a sports drink. Sports drinks are intended to be used during physical activity because they provide fluid and electrolytes. You can calculate your sweat rate by the number of pounds lost in physical activity. Each pound lost is 16 ounces of sweat; to rehydrate, you need 16 to 24 ounces of fluid.

Other things can affect hydration status. If you are used to drinking coffee or tea, you have acclimated to that level of caffeine and do not lose a significant amount of fluid. However, energy drinks can have a dehydrating effect. Alcohol stimulates the body to produce more urine, so drinking excessive amounts of alcohol can cause dehydration. Medications and disease states can cause intentional or accidental dehydration.

author bio text here Insert author bio text here Insert author bio text here Insert author bio text here Insert author bio text here Insert author bio text here Insert author bio text here Insert author bio text here Insert author bio text here Insert author bio text here Insert author bio text here Insert author bio text here

CHAPTER 14

TRUE CHEF

There is no bad cook, only lazy chefs. I would like to invite you to start cooking at home. If you can learn to shop for and prepare your own healthy meals to lose weight, you'll be more likely to reach your healthy weight. And the best part is that when you learn to cook diet-friendly meals at home, you can save money as well.

If you practice all the techniques and tools in this book, but you continue eating poorly, as in eating out five meals a day, I'm afraid the main objective of you reading this book is not achievable. You need to take control of the food that you are putting into your mouth by learning how to cook.

Eating healthily is not boring at all! When you choose to cook at home, be creative with flavors, colors, textures and spices. I always do my grocery shopping on Sunday, and I plan ahead my daily meals. Therefore, there is one thing that I always do when it comes to Friday or Saturday, when there are only enough ingredients left for one or two days: I work on my creativity to prepare something with what is left. Sometimes I'm proud to tell everyone that I'm a natural-born chef! The truth is, not me but my lovely parents are the one.

Nowadays, I think it is incredible that we have a variety of sources for inspiration when seeking for cooking ideas. My favorite sources of cooking inspiration:

Watch Cooking Videos or Shows

There are plenty of cooking shows on TV. I love watching Hell's Kitchen by Gordon Ramsay. He doesn't show you step by step how you should cook, but that's my preferred way to learn new techniques. I like to catch a few keywords when Ramsay revamps the whole menu. In this show, you are not only learning how to cook but you learn management skills as well. Kill two birds with one stone.

"Cooking is about passion, so it may look slightly temperamental in a way that it's too assertive to the naked eye." – Gordon Ramsay

YouTube is another source that I love when my mind wants to try something new! Search for "healthy meal ideas" or "how to cook quinoa," and you will get a bunch of ideas. Feel free to break the rules. That's what I mean by being creative in cooking. Do not stress yourself with all the ingredients listed out by the chef; break the rules!

Refer to Cookbooks

I only have a few printed cookbooks in my book shelf. Thanks to Google and mobile apps, you will never be short of any cooking ideas if you have a phone in hand. Some of the mobile cookbook apps you may consider are Yummly, Eat This Much, Kitchen Stories and Goodfood by BBC. One of the tricks I always do is to pick a few recipes redo them. Go for those 15-minute or 20-minute recipes if time is your main concern.

If your time allows, you can join actual cooking classes as well. I do know that some of you may want to improve your cooking skills. Taking a class with your girlfriends or partner would be a fun experience! Without you noticing, you might fall in love with cooking and it may become one of your hobbies.

Meal Prep Routine

When I'm cruising through a busy week, I will do meal prep on

Sunday, merely on cooked chicken. As for vegetables, I always want it fresh and cooked on the same day. It doesn't take much time to make garlic-fried green leafy vegetables.

The time I invest in less-than-perfect prep ahead pays off in dividends, and all I need to do is reach for something that's practically prepped and get it on the plate. This actually gives me time to eat mindfully and enjoy the taste too!

If you have a busy job, develop a reliable meal prep routine to avoid overthinking, which can lead to a downward spiral of unhelpful stress and anxiety around eating. Be flexible in what you consider a good-enough meal prep effort, given your time and money resources.

MAKE YOUR KITCHEN YOUR PLAYGROUND

You don't need a La Cornue stove, but of course, if you have the space and money, go ahead and deck out your kitchen any fancy way you want with a little herb garden in the window. Imagine having a kitchen that is well-lit, with high ceilings, combining task lighting with an ambient tone, with customized cabinetry. The surrounding environment would become inspirational and make the space feel like home while appearing natural. That is my dream kitchen!

By the way, I've made do whatever was already installed in my house. I'm perfectly good with just a frying pan and a cutting board and a knife anytime, anywhere. You do not need to spend thousands to renovate your kitchen just because you want to eat healthy. You just need the essentials:

- A stainless-steel frying pan. Look for a good heavy pan. Go for stainless-steel, not a non-sticky pan.

- A great chef's knife. A sharp and solid knife will speed up your meal prep.

• A wooden cutting board. Invest in a large, sturdy, wooden cutting board. If you have a tiny cutting board (maybe 10 inches by 6 inches) it will probably slide all over your counter, and you won't look forward to using it—or to cooking.

• An electric oven toaster. A basic one to oven bake your vegetables or meats.

• A big pot to boil in. Big enough to make soup for your whole family.

• A small pot. Small enough to cook one person's quinoa.

• A wooden spatula. One that you feel matches your frying pan will do.

Good to have:

• A slow cooker. Use it to make soup. Toss all the ingredients into the slow cooker then go off to work. When you get home, tasty soup will be waiting.

• A blender. Use it as a food processor to blend the vegetables when making soup, juices or smoothies.

• A giant refrigerator. To have enough space to keep vegetables and fruits (the one-week stocks) fresh all the time.

BUILD A HEALTHY PANTRY

Although it is entirely up to you what you keep in your pantry, there are a few food items that should be removed from your kitchen altogether. For example, instant noodles or potato chips are a problem food for many people, and even if you can turn them down, there isn't much nutritional value to them. Don't bring them into your house, and you will be happier to have made that decision. Sugar should also be eliminated from your pantry. If you have a sweet tooth, keep raw honey.

One way to improve adherence is to understand how to set up your pantry for success, and it starts with knowing some grocery shopping tips. This is one of the most fundamental concepts that sets the stage for eating healthy. If your grocery shopping is organized, it makes it so much easier for you to make better and healthier choices at home.

Make a grocery list before you go to the store. You will arrive prepared, and you will save time. Just get what you need. If it isn't on the list, don't buy it. This doesn't mean to exclude any items that you consider treats—but only buy small amounts. Remember, no restrictive diet!

A grocery list in hand also helps you think about your meals for the week, rather than just one meal or one day's meals. You have a broader perspective on your dietary choices. Making a list helps you prepare for meals in advance so that you're more likely to have a go-to option that fuels you right. If you don't use a list, especially if you are new to eating well, you are more likely to buy the food you've always bought, and that might be the problem. Use a list to remind you of the healthier choices you want to start making.

If you love to snack, store your fruits and nuts and seeds in a visible place or keep a bowl of fruit out on the counter for an easy grab-and-go option.

Simple changes to your grocery habits and kitchen setup will enable you to make better choices and help you meet your goals. Several facets of your lifestyle play a role in your ability to successfully make behavior changes, so take note of these and slowly address them over time.

TRUE CHEF

Grocery List

Whole Grains	Fish & Dairy	Fats
- Quinoa - Barley - Oats - Granola - Buckwheat - Millets - Whole wheat bread - Brown rice - 6 grains wrap	- Salmon - Saba fish - Tuna - Scallops - Shrimps - Greek yogurt - Eggs - Gallus Gallus Domesticus (Ayam Kampung)	- Extra virgin olive oil - Coconut oil
Vegetables	Fruits	Herbs, Spices & Powders
- Shitake mushrooms - Asparagus - Beans - Peas - Lentils - Seaweeds - Bell peppers - Carrots - Broccoli - Spinach - Beets - Garlic - Onion - Shallot - Cauliflower - Edamame	- Pomegranate - Raspberry - Blueberry - Strawberry - Cherry - Coconut - Pink guava - Banana - Apple - Lemon - Kiwi - Peach - Watermelon - Grapes - Passionfruit - Jackfruits	- Turmeric - Ginger - Black pepper - Saffron - Parsley - Spirulina - Lemon grass

	- Avocado	
Nuts & Seeds		**Condiments**
- Almonds - Pistachios - Walnuts - Hazelnuts - Brazil nuts	- Flaxseeds - Sesame seeds - Figs - Dates	- Chili sauce - Balsamic vinegar - Soy sauce

CHAPTER 15

MY Y.U.M. RECIPES

BREAKFAST/ LUNCH/ DINNER

- ☐ Half-boiled Eggs
- ☐ Green Eggs
- ☐ Baked Eggs in Avocado
- ☐ Muesli or Granola with Greek Yogurt
- ☐ Cereals with Greek Yogurt Topped with Pan-fried Banana
- ☐ Overnight Oats in a Jar
- ☐ Anchovy Oat Porridge
- ☐ Breakfast Burrito
- ☐ Three-Grain Porridge
- ☐ Pumpkin Millet Porridge

LUNCH/ DINNER

- Garlic Fried Basmati Rice
- Tomato Soup
- Pumpkin Soup
- Broccoli Soup
- Shrimp Aglio e Olio Spaghetti
- Oven-Baked Salmon and Asparagus
- Tofu and Kimchi Stewed
- Steam Eggs with Tofu and Shrimp
- Clay Plot Tofu with Vegetables
- Oven-Baked Chicken Legs/ Thighs
- Stir-Fried Leafy Green Vegetables
- Mussels in Ginger and Lemongrass Broth
- Chili Chicken Legs/ Thighs
- Fried Quinoa with Vegetables and Shrimps
- Fried Quinoa Vermicelli

DESSERT

- Green Beans with Ginkgo
- Sea Coconut with Dried Longan
- Pan-Fried Tapioca Cake

SNACK

- Burned Vegetables

BREAKFAST

Get the pictures of the Y.U.M. recipes on
http://www.thinkandbethin.com/

Half-Boiled Eggs

Ingredients:
Kampung Eggs
Black Pepper
Soya Sauce
Toast (optional)

proportions to taste

First put the eggs into the saucepan with enough water covering the eggs, then simmer the water without lid. Turn off the stove. Cover saucepan with lid and allow eggs to cook for 5 minutes. Remove eggs with a slotted spoon. When cool enough to handle, crack eggs into a shallow bowl. Add a little soy sauce and black pepper. Serve immediately with or without toast.

Green Eggs

Ingredients:
Eggs
Baby Spinach
Leeks
Garlic
Olive Oil
Sea Salt
Black Pepper

proportions to taste

Heat the oil in the frying pan. Add the chopped garlic; cook until golden colour. Add the sliced leeks and a pinch of salt, then cook until soft. Tip in the baby spinach and turn down the heat. Stir everything together until the spinach has wilted and reduced, then scrape it over to one side of the pan. Pour a little oil into the pan, then crack in the eggs and fry until cooked to your liking. Season with black pepper to serve.

Baked Eggs in Avocado

Ingredients:
Eggs
Avocado
Sea Salt
Black Pepper

proportions to taste

Preheat oven to 425 °F and place baking sheet or aluminium foil. Using a spoon, scoop out about two tablespoons of avocado flesh, as needed, creating a small hole in the center of each avocado. Gently crack 1 egg, and slide it into the well, keeping the yolk intact. Repeat with remaining eggs; season with salt and pepper to taste. Place into oven and bake until the egg whites have set but the yolks are still runny, about 15 minutes. Serve immediately.

Muesli or Granola with Greek Yogurt

Ingredients:
Muesli or Granola
Roasted Walnut
Flaxseed
Blended Fresh Cranberries
Greek Yogurt

Place Greek yogurt in a bowl. Add in the muesli or granola. Top with blended fresh cranberries for sweet and sour taste. Sprinkle with roasted walnut and flaxseed. Add in any other toppings you'd like (banana, berries, chia seeds, etc.). Devour!

Cereals with Greek Yogurt Topped with Pan-fried Banana

Ingredients:
Cereals
Pan-fried Banana
Greek Yogurt
Olive Oil

Slice up some ripened bananas, about 1/2" thick. Heat the oil in the frying pan and add the banana slices. Cook for a few minutes on each side until they become deeply caramelized and sticky. Place Greek yogurt in a bowl. Add in the cereal. Top with pan-fried bananas.

Overnight Oats in a Jar

Ingredients:
Rolled Oats
Mixed Berries
Unsweetened Almond Milk
Chia Seeds
Peanut Butter/ Tahini

Combine all ingredients in a lidded container or mason jar. Then refrigerate overnight. The next morning, simply stir and enjoy!

Anchovy Oats Porridge

Ingredients:
Rolled Oats
Anchovy
Walnut
Carrot
Soya Sauce
Sea Salt
Olive Oil

proportions to taste

Stir fry anchovies and boil in water. Add oats, walnut and carrots. Simmer 10 minutes. Add a pinch of salt.

Breakfast Burrito

Ingredients:
Wholegrain Wrap
Eggs
Baby Spinach
Cherry Tomatoes
Avocado
Chili Sauce (optional)
Sea Salt
Olive Oil

proportions to taste

Pour a little oil into the pan, then crack in the eggs and fry until cooked to your liking. Add the baby spinach and cherry tomatoes and turn down the heat. Add a pinch of salt. Stir everything together until the spinach has wilted and reduced. Layer everything into the centre of your wrap; top with the avocado and add some chili sauce then wrap up and eat immediately.

Three-Grain Porridge

Ingredients:
Quinoa
Millet
Buckwheat
Walnut
Dried Oyster
Turmeric Powder
Black Pepper
Soya Sauce
Sea Salt

proportions to taste

Boil quinoa, millet, buckwheat, walnut and dried oyster in saucepan for around 15 minutes. Add a pinch of turmeric powder, black pepper, salt and soy sauce to serve.

Pumpkin Millet Porridge

Ingredients:
Millet
Pumpkin
Black Pepper
Soya Sauce
Sea Salt

proportions to taste

Peel, deseed and chop the pumpkin into 1cm chunks. Steam to soften. Boil millet in saucepan. Add in the softened pumpkin to saucepan and simmer for 10 minutes. Season with black pepper to serve.

LUNCH/ DINNER

Garlic Fried Basmati Rice

Ingredients:
Basmati Rice
Eggs
Garlic
Spring Onion
Soya Sauce
Sea Salt
Olive Oil

proportions to taste

First off is to get the rice cooked. Heat the oil in the frying pan. Add the beaten eggs into the pan. Try not to let it brown. When it is nearly set, use your spatula and slice the egg into bite-sized pieces. Scoop out the egg pieces and return them to the bowl you used to beat the eggs in. They will be added back at the end. Using the same pan (no need wash), stir-fry chopped garlic until golden color, add a pinch of salt, add the rice. Put back the egg pieces. Mix everything very well until hot. Top with spring onion. Season with soy sauce to serve.

Tomato Soup

Ingredients:
Tomatoes
Onion
Garlic
Black Pepper
Sea Salt
Olive Oil

proportions to taste

Heat the oil in the frying pan. Add the chopped onion and garlic to cook until softened and starting to take on a little colour. Move to a saucepan, add a pinch of salt. Add the tomatoes and water. Bring to a simmer. Put into a glass blender and blend it to smooth. Season with black pepper to serve.

Pumpkin Soup

Ingredients:
Pumpkin
Onion
Garlic
Black Pepper
Sea Salt
Olive Oil

proportions to taste

Peel, deseed and chop the pumpkin into 1cm chunks. Steam to soften. Heat the oil in the frying pan. Add the chopped onion and garlic to cook until softened and starting to take on a little colour. Add a pinch of salt. Put the steamed pumpkin and the fried onion and garlic into a glass blender and blend it to smooth. Pour back into a saucepan. Bring to a simmer. Season with black pepper to serve.

Broccoli Soup

Ingredients:
Broccoli
Onion
Garlic
Black Pepper
Sea Salt
Olive Oil

proportions to taste

Cut broccoli into pieces and steam to soften. Heat the oil in the frying pan. Add the chopped onion and garlic to cook until softened and starting to take on a little colour. Add a pinch of salt. Put the steamed broccoli and the fried onion and garlic into a glass blender and blend it to smooth. Pour back into a saucepan. Bring to a simmer. Season with black pepper to serve.

Shrimp Aglio e Olio Spaghetti

Ingredients:
Whole-Wheat Spaghetti
Shrimp
Parsley
Garlic
Red Pepper Flakes
Sea Salt
Olive Oil

proportions to taste

Bring a pot of water to boil. Cook the spaghetti according to the package instructions. Drain and wash with normal temperature water and set aside. Heat a frying pan on medium heat and add the olive oil. Add the garlic and sauté for 30 seconds, add the shrimp, chili flakes and salt. Cook the shrimp until both sides turn white, then add the spaghetti and water into the pan. Stir to combine well. Add the parsley into the pan, stir to distribute well. Turn off the heat. Dish out and serve immediately.

Oven-Baked Salmon and Asparagus

Ingredients:
Salmon
Asparagus
Lemon
Rosemary
Sea Salt
Black Pepper
Olive Oil

proportions to taste

Snap off the woody ends of the asparagus. Layer asparagus in a lightly buttered baking dish; spray with cooking spray and season with salt and pepper. Next, arrange the salmon fillets over the asparagus; set aside. Season with salt and pepper, rub all over the salmon fillets. Top salmon with lemon slices and fresh rosemary. Bake at 400°F for 17 to 20 minutes, or until fish flakes easily and asparagus is fork tender. For a light crisp and browned top, I suggest to pop it under the broiler for the last 3 to 4 minutes. Watch it closely and do not overcook.
Squeeze some lemon juice over the salmon, add fresh herbs if you'd like, and serve.

Tofu and Kimchi Stewed

Ingredients:
Tofu
Kimchi
Radish
Spring Onion
Garlic
Ginger
Olive Oil

proportions to taste

Heat oil in a large saucepan over high. Cook white and pale-green parts of spring onion, garlic, and ginger, stirring often, until softened and fragrant, about 3 minutes. Add water. Add daikon and gently simmer until daikon is tender, 15–20 minutes. Add kimchi and tofu. Simmer until tofu is heated through. Serve.

Steam Eggs with Tofu and Shrimp

```
Ingredients:
Tofu
Shrimp
Eggs
Spring Onion
Sea Salt
Soy Sauce

proportions to taste
```

Cut and place the tofu pieces in the deep plate. Cut the cleaned shrimp into small pieces and place on tofu. Beat the eggs well with salt. Slowly add the same amount of warm water to the egg and beat well and pour into the plate. Steam for around 10 minutes. Season with a little of soy sauce. Sprinkle spring onion on top to serve.

Clay Pot Tofu with Vegetables

```
Ingredients:
Tofu
Bamboo Shoot
Button Mushroom
Cloud Fungus
Cabbage
Snow Peas
Garlic
Ginger
Sea Salt
Soy Sauce
Cornstarch Slurry
Olive Oil

proportions to taste
```

Cut the tofu into slices or pieces at least 1 cm thick. Smaller pieces tend to break easily. Pan-fry the tofu in a saucepan until it turns golden brown. Remove and set aside. Heat some oil in the pan to sauté the garlic and sliced ginger. Once they turn aromatic, add all the button mushrooms and vegetables and stir fry briefly. The sequence of adding the vegetables is not critical. The only exception is not to braise the snow peas to preserve their crunchiness. Transfer the vegetables to a clay pot. Add the water and the seasonings (salt and soy sauce) to braise the vegetables for five minutes. You can cover the pan/clay pot or leave it open if there is too much liquid after braising for five minutes. Add some cornstarch slurry to thicken the sauce so that it will cling to the vegetables. The cornstarch slurry should consist of one part of cornstarch and two parts of water. Add the slurry and mix with the vegetables in batches and discard the remaining once you get the right consistency. The sauce will be too thick and gooey if you add too much cornstarch slurry. Ready to serve.

Oven-Baked Chicken Legs/ Thighs

Ingredients:
Chicken Legs / Thighs
Shallot
Sea Salt
Olive Oil

proportions to taste

Mash the shallots using mortar and pestle. Then squeeze out the shallot juice using hands; you can throw away the fibres. Coat the chicken legs or thighs with salt and olive oil, and pour in the shallot juice. Marinate for 40 minutes. Bake at 425 °F for 20 minutes, then flip to the other side for 15 minutes. Serve.

Stir-Fried Leafy Green Vegetables

Ingredients:
Sweet Potato Leaves/ Watercress/ Kale/
Spinach/ Mustard Greens
Garlic
Sea Salt
Olive Oil

proportions to taste

Heat the oil in the wok/ pan. Sauté the garlic until fragrant over low heat. Add the salt. Add the blanched vegetables. Stir-fried over high heat until it turns fragrant. Dish out and serve.

Mussels in Ginger and Lemongrass Broth

Ingredients:
Mussels
Lemon
Garlic
Ginger
Sea Salt
Olive Oil

proportions to taste

Heat the oil in the wok/ pan. Sauté the garlic until fragrant over low heat. Add the salt. Add the blanched vegetables. Stir-fry over high heat until it turns fragrant. Dish out and serve.

Chili Chicken Legs/ Thighs

Ingredients:
Chicken Legs/ Thighs
Shallots
Chili Boh
Lemongrass
Sea Salt
Olive Oil

proportions to taste

Marinate the chicken with a pinch of salt. Fry at the optimal range of 350 °F to 375 °F and do not overcrowd the pan to prevent the temperature from plummeting. Drain instead on a wire rack set over a baking sheet or in a metal colander set over a bowl. Next stir-fry the chopped shallots with lemongrass until fragrant before adding the chili boh. Lastly, put the fried-chicken back to the pan and add 200ml water to cook for 10 minutes. Dish out and serve.

Fried Quinoa with Vegetables and Shrimp

Ingredients:
Quinoa
Zucchini
Cilantro
Eggs
Shrimp
Sea Salt
Soy Sauce
Olive Oil

proportions to taste

Cook quinoa and set aside. Sauté zucchini and set aside. Scramble and cook eggs and add a pinch of salt. Add in shrimp. Add quinoa and cook briefly with soy sauce. Add in sautéed zucchini. Toss in cilantro and serve warm.

Fried Quinoa Vermicelli

```
Ingredients:
Quinoa Vermicelli
Cilantro
Eggs
Shrimp
Sea Salt
Soy Sauce
Olive Oil

proportions to taste
```

Scramble and cook eggs and add a pinch of salt. Add in shrimp. Add in quinoa vermicelli and cook briefly with soy sauce. Toss in cilantro and serve warm.

DESSERTS

Green Bean with Ginkgo

```
Ingredients:
Green Bean
Ginkgo
Dried Orange/Tangerine Peel
Pandan Leaves
Honey

proportions to taste
```

In a soup pot, add green beans, pandan leaves, water and orange peel. Bring to a boil. Add gingko and reduce heat to a simmer, partially covered, for about 50 minutes (or until the beans are soft), stirring the sides and bottom of the pot occasionally. Top up with hot water at any time if needed. Discard orange peel slices and pandan leaves. Add the amount of honey to taste. Serve warmed or chilled.

Sea Coconut with Dried Longan

Ingredients:
Sea Coconut
Dried Longan
Pandan leaves
Honey

proportions to taste

Peel off the light brown skin of the sea coconuts and slice them into thin slices. In a large pot, put in all the ingredients (except honey) and bring to boil. Turn to low heat and continue to simmer for 45 minutes to 1 hour. Add honey (optional as the broth tastes sweet enough from the dried Longan) and serve.

Pan-Fried Tapioca Cake

Ingredients:
Tapioca Root
Freshly Squeezed Coconut Milk
Brown Sugar
Fresh Pandan Extract
Olive Oil

proportions to taste

Put all ingredients (except olive oil) in a big mixing bowl and stir well. You can use your hand to mix; if possible, use a food processor instead. The food processor is able to further refine the batter and ensure it is well mixed to give the cake a better texture. Transfer to a baking tin and steam under high heat in a steamer for at least 25-30 minutes or until a skewer inserted comes out clean. The steaming time will depend on the size of your baking tin used. It is best for the skewer test be done on separate places in the cake, especially the centre. Ensure there is enough water throughout the steaming period. Cool completely (possibly for 1-2 hours) before cutting. You may serve it now or pan-fry it. Heat up a pan with one tsp of oil and put the cut tapioca cake into the pan. Let it cook for a minute till crispy and turn over to cook the other side.

SNACKS

Burned Vegetables

Ingredients:
Sweet Potato, peeled
Beet, peeled
Kale
Brussels Sprouts
Olive Oil
Sea Salt
proportions to taste

Root Vegetables (Beet and Sweet Potato)

Preheat oven to 200°F (95°C) and place the oven rack in the centre of the oven. Use a food processor to slice the veggies consistently as thinly as possible (1/16 inch/1.6 mm at the most). This will ensure even baking and crispness. If you have some ninja skills, you can also use a sharp knife. For extra crispness, soak the sweet potatoes in cold water for 10-20 minutes to help release the starch from the potatoes. Once soaked, rinse the sweet potatoes under cold running water. Spread the veggies onto a paper towel and pat them dry. Place them into a large bowl. Add oil and salt. Toss well. Let the veggies sweat for about 15 minutes until they release their natural juices. Then drain off any excess liquid. Place the veggies into a single layer onto parchment paper (or an oven rack). Make sure the veggies aren't touching. Bake for 30 minutes at 200°F. Then increase the temperature to 220°F, rotate the parchment paper/oven rack, and bake for an additional 30 minutes. Be sure to watch closely past the 45-minute mark as the chips can burn quickly. Allow to cool.

Leafy Vegetables (Kale and Brussels Sprouts)

Preheat oven to 200°F and place the oven rack in the centre of the oven. Tear kale away from the stem and roughly tear it up into large pieces. Remove the leaves of the Brussels sprouts. Wash and spin the leaves until thoroughly dry. If you don't have a spinner, place the leaves in a large bowl and cover them with water. Let them soak for a few minutes to allow any dirt to sink to the bottom of the bowl. Place the leaves onto a paper towel and pat them dry. Transfer the leaves into a large bowl and massage in the oil and salt. Place the veggies into a single layer onto parchment paper (or an oven rack). Make sure the veggies aren't touching. Bake for about 45 minutes until the leaves are dry and crispy. Rotate the parchment paper/oven rack halfway through baking. Be sure to watch closely past the 30-minute mark as they can burn quickly. Allow to cool.

Source of my organic ingredients: Love Earth Organic

Organic Black Pepper Powder	Brown Sugar
Sea Salt	Millet
Muesli or Granola	Buckwheat
Roasted Walnut	Walnut
Flaxseed	Turmeric Powder
Cereals	Red Pepper Flakes
Rolled Oats	Cornstarch Slurry
Chia Seeds	Green Bean
Quinoa	Ginkgo
Basmati Rice	

MAKING IT HAPPEN

CHAPTER 16

START CREATING YOUR NEW BODY

Think and Be T.H.I.N. Transformation Blueprint can be done in a 12-week plan. As you will see, it's pretty easy to do and becomes ingrained into your daily life. Once it becomes part of your life, it will run on autopilot mode.

The Approach Week by Week

Week 1	Set a realistic goal and plan ahead.
	THINK Watch your river of thoughts (Chapter 1) Don't judge, write down all your thoughts in a journal. Put them into two categories. One group is supporting your goal, one is working against your goal.
	HYBRID HIIT 3 Cardio sessions 1 Upper body workout 1 Lower body workout 1 Abs workout 1 Long circuit (Refer to 12-week HYBRID HIIT workout plan in

	Chapter 9) Kickstart your workout. If you have a medical condition, you may practice the 5-day slow walk (Refer to Get Out of Your Comfort Zone in Chapter 7). **SURVIVAL INSTINCT** Acknowledge the damage of dieting (Refer to kNOwing Dieting Mentality in Chapter 12). **NUTRITION** Do a quick check on what you have in your pantry; list it out. Categorize your food into highest quality, medium quality and low quality (Refer to Highest, Medium and Lowest Strategies in Chapter 13).
Week 2-3	**THINK** Practice Three Steps to Visualize Yourself Thin (Refer to Visualize Yourself Thin in Chapter 2); do this early in the morning and before you go to bed at night. For starters, download the guided visualization audio at http://www.thinkandbethin.com/. **HYBRID HIIT** (Refer to 12-Week HYBRID HIIT Workout Plan in Chapter 9) **SURVIVAL INSTINCT** Keep a journal to define the following feeling and behaviors: When are you triggered to eat? What are triggered to eat? Why are you triggered to eat? What do you end up eating? How do you eat? How do you feel when you eat? How do you feel directly after you have eaten? How do you feel 2 hours after you've eaten? How do you feel the day after you have eaten? We are using this process purely to learn about yourself.

	NUTRITION Use this one week to check on how many times you eat out. Plan and prepare more meals at home to keep from eating out too often.

Week 4-5	**THINK** Review your thoughts journal in Week 1. It's time for a game! Have fun interrupting the patterns (negative thoughts). You may use any ridiculous words you can (Refer to Form New Beliefs in Chapter 2). Continue to practice visualization 2 times a day. **HYBRID HIIT** Use mantras to push yourself forward (Refer to Chapter 8: magic of Mantra- Mind Over Body). (Refer to 12-Week HYBRID HIIT Workout Plan in Chapter 9) **SURVIVAL INSTINCT** Be aware of your hunger and fullness scale (Refer to Practicing Food Mindfulness in Chapter 10). Eat when you are hungry, not because of fake hunger in your mind. **NUTRITION** Work on a healthy grocery list and eat real food (Refer to Food Without Label in Chapter 13 and Build a Healthy Pantry in Chapter 14). Your grocery list should consist of highest quality food. Always bring your list to the store; do not grab things that are not on the list.

Week 6-7	**THINK**
	You have identified your negative thoughts/ beliefs, used words power to interrupt patterns. You can now reinforce a new belief by following the Three Steps to Form New Beliefs (Refer to Form New Beliefs in Chapter 2).
	Keep reminding yourself.
	Continue to practice visualization 2 times a day.
	HYBRID HIIT
	(Refer to 12-Week HYBRID HIIT Workout Plan in Chapter 9)
	SURVIVAL INSTINCT
	Implement B.A.M. principles (Refer to Practicing Food Mindfulness in Chapter 10).
	Continue paying attention to your hunger and fullness scale.
	NUTRITION
	You bought highest quality real food from the store in Week 3. It is time to be your own chef! Pick up some essentials you need for cooking. Refer to True Chef and Make Your Kitchen Your Playground in Chapter 14.
	If you happen to eat out, let's say for lunch due to work, please choose to eat 80% clean.

Week 8-9	**THINK**
	Identify one eating habit you need to change this week using Carrot Trick to Build Good Eating Habits/ Exercise Habits (Refer to Carrot Trick in Chapter 4).
	Continue to work on your new beliefs; you will need

time to shift your old beliefs and make them unfamiliar (Refer to Form New Beliefs - Making the Unfamiliar (New Beliefs) Familiar in Chapter 2).

Continue to practice visualization 2 times a day.

HYBRID HIIT
Do not press your pause-button. Continue to progress and do not aim for perfection (Refer to Pause-Button Mentality in Chapter 7).
(Refer to 12-Week HYBRID HIIT Workout Plan in Chapter 9)

SURVIVAL INSTINCT
Make peace with food by improving your nutrition knowledge (Refer to Making Peace with Food in Chapter 10 and Highest, Medium and Lowest Strategies – Protein Power, Carbs the Enemy and Fat Facts in Chapter 13).
Continue paying attention to your hunger and fullness scale and implementing B.A.M. principles.

NUTRITION
Eat five meals a day as breakfast, lunch, dinner and two snacks and sometimes desserts (Refer to Chapter 15 MY Y.U.M Recipes). Stop as soon as you feel full, and eat again whenever you like.

Week 10-11	**THINK** Forming one new habit (body movement, meditation, gratitude journaling) using Fogg Behavior Model (Refer to Tiny Habits in Chapter 3). Also refer to Tune Up Your Brain with Mediation and Power of Gratitude in Chapter 4. Continue to practice visualization 2 times a day. **HYBRID HIIT** Pain Is Mental- Chapter 7 (Refer to 12-Week HYBRID HIIT Workout Plan in Chapter 9) **SURVIVAL INSTINCT** Change your self-talk, alter your thinking, and delete your inner critics. Learn to love yourself and honour your body (Refer to Chapter 11: The Compassionate Instinct). To have more me time and do just one thing at a time (Refer to My She Shed and Do JUST 1 Thing in Chapter 4). Continue paying attention to your hunger and fullness scale and implement B.A.M. principles. **NUTRITION** Keep yourself hydrated (Refer to Stay Hydrated in Chapter 13).

Week 12	**THINK** You have trained your mind thin! Challenge yourself to form new habits after you conquer one and have it on autopilot mode. Enhance your healthy lifestyle by connecting to Mother Nature and sleep more to manage your stress (Refer to Chapter 5: Connecting to Mother Nature and Chapter 6: Sleep more, Stress Less). Continuously form new beliefs and interrupt old belief patterns using word power. Continue to practice visualization 2 times a day. (By now, you should have trained yourself to visualize yourself thin anytime anywhere). **HYBRID HIIT** Your body is toned up now! (Refer to 12-Week HYBRID HIIT Workout Plan in Chapter 9) **SURVIVAL INSTINCT** You have learned your way thin! You have reprogrammed your brain! **NUTRITION** You are eating your way thin! You enjoy high-quality real food.

My memories of seeing my parents coming in wet from the morning vegetables pick in the very early days of farming are still fresh and clear. Even now, after living in the city of Kuala Lumpur, I still think of myself as a farm girl or village girl, happiest when I'm around chilis and bugs and rivers. My parents There is no bad cook, only lazy chefs. I wou

CHAPTER 17

HOW FAST WILL I SEE RESULTS?

Think and Be T.H.I.N. is not a diet program. The allure of all diets is how quickly you'll lose weight. But why is it that nobody ever talks about the rebound effect that happens after you go off a diet program? Why does everybody see it as normal to jump from one diet to another or to keep trying the same diet over and over again. Think and Be T.H.I.N. is not a diet program that you need to jump on when you want to get your ideal body, and press the pause-button when you need a break. Think and Be T.H.I.N. is a systematic approach that caters every aspect (mindset, body movement, instinct, and nutrition) by: -

● Using tools to break your mental barriers due to your good or bad experiences.
● Introducing the most effective body movements to tone your body.
● Understanding the survival instinct.
● Sharing nutritional knowledge.

If being overweight or obese has been a lifetime struggle for you and you've tried dieting for a long period, it will take some time to undo the diet mentality. The most important thing is to empty your cup so you can learn faster and see results. If you have tried to starve yourself in order to shed some pounds, you might gain some weight when you start to eat normal. However, after a few weeks, you will find yourself eating healthier by making peace with food. You are not going to restrict yourself (no calorie counting, no weighing food), and you will naturally crave nutritious food like vegetables and fruits. You understand the survival instinct and only eat when you are hungry.

After all, this system never promises that you will not experience plateaus. Shedding pounds is not linear. Your weight will fluctuate on a day-to-day basis if you are the type who loves to weigh-in on a daily basis. There will be days your scale weight goes up. There will be days your scale weight goes down. And there will be days your scale weight does not change. For many of us, a scale is a dangerous tool, but only when we are not familiar with why we have "gained weight" according to the scale. On a day-to-day basis, the scale can fluctuate quite a bit, but it does not mean you have put on fat. You see, the scale measures weight. That weight consists of how much food you have in your stomach, how much water you've drunk, how much your bones weigh, how much your muscles weigh, and how much water your body is retaining. One significant component that causes such fluctuation on a day-to-day basis is the latter regarding how much water you're retaining due to eating more carbs and sodium than usual and even physical/mental/emotional stress.

When you look at progress over time, keep in mind that both your muscles and your bones weigh more as your strength train. Other reasons your scale can fluctuate can depend on if you haven't been sleeping very well, if your digestion is off, or even if you are experiencing your menstrual cycle (for females). I hope this helps you understand that when you see the scale rise, it doesn't always mean you've gained fat.

You are human, and you should expect these variations, and by projecting these differences, you will have a more successful journey.

FOCUS ON YOUR HEALTH, NOT YOUR BODY WEIGHT! THROW AWAY YOUR SCALE!

Think and Be T.H.I.N. Transformation Blueprint is an approach to change your mindset to change your body, but most importantly to reclaim your lean, strong and confident body and beyond, which doesn't have an endpoint, and doesn't use the scales as the sole judge of success. No million-dollar paycheck required!

TESTIMONIALS

Jennifer T., 39

"Your program jumpstart healthy change in my life."

Jennifer is a teacher for special care education. I bet you can imagine her patience in taking care of special kids from 9 to 5. Most of the time she would just ignore her meals, simply grab something to put into her mouth or what not, and continue the busy day ahead! She is also not an active person, the most she would do is a slow walk in her residential area. She once told me that even her dad is far better than her, who does his morning walk in the park daily, around 4:00 am! One day, she did her medical checkup. Looking at her medical report, her doctor told her to pay attention to her blood pressure, which had exceeded the normal range for her age. Hence, due to that alarm, she found my online program. As I mentioned in the book as well as to her, my program is not a quick-fix diet plan. She needed to change her mind in order to change her body.

"I want to truly thank you for your support with everything. Prior to attending your online program, I had tried a 90-day restrictive diet program and failed. It was easier to ignore taking care of my mind and body and to focus on work. Today I can truly say I put me first before everything else. What I like the most about Grace's program is the visualization session, which really pushed me forward for not ignoring my health. Your program jumpstarted a healthy change in my life." --Jennifer

Cath O., 54

"Ability to make conscious food choices"

Cath is a retired finance personnel and enjoys her wifey lifestyle. "I don't cook a lot, and my son likes Western food, so we eat out like three times a week and therefore I eat a lot of fried stuff," Cath told me during our assessment session. She was not happy with her tummy fat. However, she loved taking brisk walks in the park most of the time. She was in decent health, without any issues. Her goal was to lose fat and tone up her body.

"I picked up new knowledge from Grace's online program and I feel confident in my ability to make conscious food choices, especially when eating out. I know that it is totally within my control to continue this journey and relationship with food. As I have become more mindful, I've started to take note of how my body looks and I realize that my standing posture needs to be corrected. I started to take note of how my body looks as well as my body posture. I also practice the hunger fullness scale by eating only 70% full. I totally agree with what Grace said to think positive and visualize the outcome. Focus on the outcome, and do not get stuck in your current self. I want to thank you so much for your guidance and love through this process. The tools you offered me and your unwavering support have given me more than I could've ever dreamt." --Cath

START CREATING YOUR NEW BODY

Chris K., 50

Chris is an entrepreneur in the wellness industry. She reached out to me after seeing my content on social media. We kicked off a 1:1 coaching with the objective to cultivate a healthy lifestyle.

Chris, "Actually, after these 2 weeks of new adjustment
- my digestive system is better
- my period cycle is better, pre-menopausal symptoms have improved a bit
- my skin is smoother (I sweat a lot)."

"Grace walks the talk to maintain her lean, strong and confident body shape. She shows consistent passion about engagement on sports and balanced eating."

"My best takeaways are: -
- settling a right mindset of why I want to change to a healthy lifestyle.
- set the little implementing effort every day, like after sending off my son to school, I would go for a short hike or a 30-minute brisk walk at the park.
- understand what real food is, a new shopping list in my weekly routine.
- eating my food in the right proportion, that can be applied anyway I go; my social gathering with friend is going as usual, as long as I am aware of the portions taken.
- this program is a sustainable approach; I have confidence that I will able to carry on with it after the program.
- learned some new recipes that are suitable with Chinese style."

"How I feel after the coaching:
- I am less tired and have more energy after eating real food, for example, millet porridge, oat porridge, brown rice noodles, etc.
- cultivating an exercise routine and eating healthy helped me to cope with my pre-menopausal symptoms in a better way."

REFERENCES

Aleeze´ Sattar Moss., et al., "Effects of an 8-Week Meditation Program on Mood and Anxiety in Patients with Memory Loss" *The Journal of Alternative and Complementary Medicine* Volume 18, Number 1, 2012, pp. 48–53

American Diabetes Association. "Glycemic Index and Diabetes." http://www.diabetes.org/food-and-fitness/food/what-can-i-eat/understandingcarbohydrates/glycemic-index-and-diabetes.html.

American Heart Association. "Monounsaturated Fats." http://www.heart.org/HEARTORG/GettingHealthy/NutritionCenter/HealthyEating/Monounsaturated-Fats_UCM_301460_Article.jsp#.

Anna Kramer, These 10 Companies Make a Lot of the Food We Buy. Here's How We Made Them Better. 2014. Oxfam America. https://www.oxfamamerica.org/explore/stories/these-10-companies-make-a-lot-of-the-food-we-buy-heres-how-we-made-them-better/

Brouns, F., and W. Saris. "How Vitamins Affect Performance." *The Journal of Sports Medicine and Physical Fitness* 29, no. 4 (1989): 400–404.

Buchanan K, Sheffield J. "Why do diets fail? An exploration of dieters' experiences using thematic analysis." *J Health Psychol.* 2017 Jun;22(7):906-915. doi:10.1177/1359105315618000. Epub 2015 Dec 16. PMID: 26679713. https://pubmed.ncbi.nlm.nih.gov/26679713/

Calton, Jayson B. "Prevalence of Micronutrient Deficiency in Popular Diet Plans." *Journal of the International Society of Sports Nutrition* 7 (2010): 1–9.

Canetti, et al., Analysis of How a Child's Eating Instincts "Foods and Emotion." *Behavioural Processes* 60 2 (2002): 157–64.

Does Your Subconscious Mind Control Your Dreams?: https://www.thewisdompost.com/law-of-attraction/subconscious-

mind/does-your-subconscious-mind-control-your-
dreams/1003#how-does-your-subconscious-mind-works

Dunham, Will. "Weight of the World: 2.1 Billion People Obese or
Overweight." *Reuters*.
http://www.reuters.com/article/2014/05/28/ushealth- obesity-
idUSKBN0E82HX20140528.

Evelyn Tribole, MS, RD, and Elyse Resch, MS, RD, FADA (2003)
"Intuitive Eating: A Revolutionary Program That Works"

F. Marijn Stok, Emely De Vet, Jane Wardle, Maria T. Chu, John De
Wit, Denise T.D. De Ridder, "Navigating the obesogenic
environment: How psychological sensitivity to the food environment
and self-regulatory competence are associated with adolescent
unhealthy snacking," *Eating Behaviors*, Volume 17, 2015, Pages 19-22,
ISSN 1471-0153, https://doi.org/10.1016/j.eatbeh.2014.12.003.
https://www.sciencedirect.com/science/article/pii/S1471015314001
755

Factors, Coronary Heart Disease, Stroke, and Diabetes: A Fresh
Look at the
Evidence." *Lipids* 45, no. 10 (2010): 893–905. Available at
http://www.ncbi.nlm.nih.gov/pubmed/20354806.

Folch, N., et al. "Metabolic Response to a Large Starch Meal after
Rest and Exercise: Comparison between Men and Women." *European
Journal of Clinical Nutrition* 57, no. 9 (2003): 1107–1115.

Folch, N., et al. "Metabolic Response to Small and Large 13 C-
Labelled Pasta Meals Following Rest or Exercise in Man." *British
Journal of Nutrition* 85 (2001): 671–680.

France Bellisle, Meals and snacking, diet quality and energy balance,
Physiology & Behavior, Volume 134, 2014, Pages 38-43, ISSN 0031-
9384, https://doi.org/10.1016/j.physbeh.2014.03.010.
https://www.sciencedirect.com/science/article/pii/S0031938414001
449

Fuentes Artiles, et al., Mindful Eating and Common Diet Programs Lower Body Weight Similarly: Systematic Review and Meta-Analysis, Obesity Reviews, 2019:20:1619-1627., DOI: 10.1111/obr.12918. https://onlinelibrary-wileycom.stanford.idm.oclc.org/doi/epdf/10.1111/obr.12918

Gardner, F.L. & Moore, Z.E. (2007). The Psychology of Enhancing Human Performance" The Mindfulness-acceptance-commitment (MAC) Approach. New York: Springer Publishing Company. https://www.spring.org.uk/2009/09/how-long-to-form-a-habit.php

Genes are not destiny
https://www.hsph.harvard.edu/obesity-prevention-source/obesity-causes/genes-and-obesity/

Greer, B. K., et al. "Branched-Chain Amino Acid Supplementation and Indicators of Muscle Damage after Endurance Exercise." *International Journal of Sports Nutrition and Exercise Metabolism* 17, no. 6 (2007): 595–607.

Hall et al., *Ultra-Processed Diets Cause Excess Calorie Intake and Weight Gain: An Inpatient Randomized Controlled Trial of Ad Libitum Food Intake.* 2019, Cell Metabolism 30, 67-77. 02 July 2019. Published by Elsevier Inc. https://doi.org/10.1016/j.cmet.2019.05.008. https://www.cell.com/cell-metabolism/pdf/S1550-4131(19)30248-7.pdf

Harvard Health Publications. "Glycemic Index and Glycemic Load for 100+ Foods." http://www.health.harvard.edu/newsweek/Glycemic_index_and_glycemic_load_for_100_foods.htm.

Holt, S. H., et al. "An Insulin Index of Foods: The Insulin Demand Generated by 1000-kJ Portions of Common Foods." *American Journal of Clinical Nutrition* 66, no. 5 (1997): 1264–1276.

"Hydration Needs and Tips—Staying Hydrated and Rehydrating": http://www.mckinley.uiuc.edu/Handouts/hydrate_needs_exercise.html

Iowa State University Extension and Outreach. "Fat." http://www.extension.iastate.edu/humansciences/fat.

J. W. Fielding, "Adjunct Chemotherapy in Operable Gastric Cancer," *Worla Jour- nai oj Surgery* 7, no. 3 (1983).

Jessica Christine Kwik (2008). Traditional Food Knowledge: Renewing Culture and Restoring Health. UWSpace. http://hdl.handle.net/10012/4052

Jon Kabat-Zinn. Full Catastrophe Living. (1990). Delta:NY,NY.

Kesten, D,. et al., "Whole-person Integrative Eating: A Program for Treating Overeating, Overweight, and Obesity." *Integrative Medicine: A Clinician's Journal.* 2015 Oct; 14(5): 42–50. Available from: https://www.ncbi.nlm.nih.gov/pmc/articles/PMC4712862/

Kim E. Innes , et al., Volume 2018 | Article ID 7683897 | https://doi.org/10.1155/2018/7683897 "Effects of Mantra Meditation versus Music Listening on Knee Pain, Function, and Related Outcomes in Older Adults with Knee Osteoarthritis: An Exploratory Randomized Clinical Trial (RCT)" Available from: https://www.hindawi.com/journals/ecam/2018/7683897/

Kristeller, J. L., & Epel, E. (2014). *Mindful eating and mindless eating: The science and the practice.* In A. le, C. T. Ngnoumen, & E. J. Langer (Eds.), *The Wiley Blackwell handbook of mindfulness* (p. 913–933). Wiley Blackwell. https://doi.org/10.1002/9781118294895.ch47

Lacoste-Badie S, Minvielle M, Droulers O. "Attention to food health warnings in children's advertising: a French perspective." *Public Health.* 2019 Aug;173:69-74. doi: 10.1016/j.puhe.2019.05.012. Epub 2019 Jun 27. PMID: 31254680.

Maslow, A. H. (1943). A theory of human motivation. *Psychological Review, 50*(4), 370–396. https://doi.org/10.1037/h0054346

Mayo Oshin, 5 hidden causes of stress and anxiety
https://www.theladders.com/career-advice/5-hidden-causes-of-stress-and-anxiety

Meredith, C. N., et al. "Dietary Protein Requirements and Body Protein Metabolism in Endurance-Trained Men." *Journal of Applied Physiology* 66, no. 6 (1989): 2850–2856.

Micha, R., and D. Mozzaffarian. "Saturated Fat and Cardiometabolic Risk

Nan Lu, OMD with Ellen Schaplowsky, "Digesting the Universe: A Revolutionary Framework for Healthy Metabolism Function."

Neff KD. "The development and validation of a scale to measure self-compassion." *Self Identity*. 2003;2:223–250. [Google Scholar]

Niall McCarthy, Where People Spend The Most Time Eating and Drinking, Statista.com, 31 July 2020.
https://www.statista.com/chart/13226/where-people-spend-the-most-time-eating-drinking/

O'Mahony, M. (1986), "Sensory Adaptation. Journal of Sensory Studies," 1: 237-258. https://doi.org/10.1111/j.1745-459X.1986.tb00176.x

Olson, Michele Ph.D., FACSM, CSCS. ACSM's Health & Fitness Journal: September/October 2014 - Volume 18 - Issue 5 - p 17-24

Patton E. Burchett., The 'Magical' Language of Mantra *Journal of the American Academy of Religion*, Volume 76, Issue 4, December 2008, Pages 807–843, https://doi.org/10.1093/jaarel/lfn089

Phillippa Lally, Cornelia H. M. van Jaarsveld, Henry W. W. Potts & Jane Wardle. (2009). "How are habits formed: Modelling habit formation in the real world." *European Journal of social Psychology*. https://doi.org/10.1002/ejsp.674

Rahimi Ardabili, Hania & Reynolds, Rebecca & Vartanian, Lenny & McLeod, Leigh & Zwar, Nicholas. (2018). A Systematic Review of the Efficacy of Interventions that Aim to Increase Self-Compassion on Nutrition Habits, Eating Behaviours, Body Weight and Body Image. Mindfulness. 9. 1-13. 10.1007/s12671-017-0804-0.

S. A. Giduck, "Cephalic Reflexes: Their Role in Digestion and Possible Roles in Absorption and Metabolism," *Journal of Nutrition* 117, no. 7 (July 1987).

Schulte EM, Avena NM, Gearhardt AN (2015) Which Foods May Be Addictive? The Roles of Processing, Fat Content, and Glycemic Load. PLoS ONE 10(2): e0117959. https://doi.org/10.1371/journal.pone.0117959

Shepherd, G. Smell images and the flavour system in the human brain. *Nature* **444,** 316–321 (2006). https://doi.org/10.1038/nature05405

Simopoulos, A. P. "The Importance of the Ratio of Omega-6/Omega-3 Essential Fatty Acids." *Biomedical and Pharmaceutical* 56, no. 8 (2002): 365–379. Available at http://www.ncbi.nlm.nih.gov/pubmed/12442909.

Srour, et al., *Ultra-processed food intake and risk of cardiovascular disease: prospective cohort study (NutriNet-Santé)* BMJ 2019; 365 doi: https://doi.org/10.1136/bmj.l1451 (Published 29 May 2019). https://www.bmj.com/content/365/bmj.l1451

Steve Bradt, "Wandering mind not a happy mind" https://news.harvard.edu/gazette/story/2010/11/wandering-mind-not-a-happy-mind/

Stress and Sleep https://www.apa.org/news/press/releases/stress/2013/sleep

"Tabata vs HIIT: Which Burns More Fat?" https://skinnyms.com/tabata-vs-hiit-which-burns-more-fat/

Tarnopolsky, M. A., et al. "Evaluation of Protein Requirements for Trained Strength Athletes." *Journal of Applied Physiology* 73, no. 5 (1992): 1986–1995.

The Center for Mindful Eating website: http://www.tcme.org/

Top 5 Exercises To Activate Your Subconscious Mind: https://www.thewisdompost.com/law-of-attraction/subconscious-mind/top-5-exercises-to-activate-your-subconscious-mind/1007

Turning Stress into an Asset https://hbr.org/2011/06/turning-stress-into-an-asset

Tylka, T. 2006. Development and psychometric evaluation of a measure of intuitive eating. Journal of Counseling Psychology 53:226-240.

Wang, Y., Beydoun, M.A., Liang, L., Caballero, B. and Kumanyika, S.K. (2008), Will All Americans Become Overweight or Obese? Estimating the Progression and Cost of the US *Obesity Epidemic. Obesity*, 16: 2323 2330. https://doi.org/10.1038/oby.2008.351. https://onlinelibrary.wiley.com/doi/full/10.1038/oby.2008.351

Wiss DA, Avena N and Rada P (2018) Sugar Addiction: From Evolution to Revolution. *Front. Psychiatry* 9:545. doi: 10.3389/fpsyt.2018.00545

Wiss, David A et al. "Sugar Addiction: From Evolution to Revolution." *Frontiers in psychiatry* vol. 9 545. 7 Nov. 2018, doi:10.3389/fpsyt.2018.00545

Yang, Quanhe, et al. "Added Sugar Intake and Cardiovascular Diseases Mortality among U.S. Adults." *JAMA Internal Medicine* 174, no. 4 (2014): 516–524. http://www.hsph.harvard.edu/nutritionsource/what-should-you-eat/carbohydrates-full-story/index.html.

Visit the Website to attend THIN Transformation LIVE Masterclass:

https://www.thinkandbethin.com/

Made in the USA
Middletown, DE
20 March 2022